Comments on Gerard Malanga's Poetry

Now and again a poet is found who is a complex of many capabilities and patterns, all relating but none so isolating in its practice that the one is lost to the other. I have marveled for years at Gerard Malanga's articulate endurance as a poet—and also as a photographer of singular power. He has moved with deftness and great authority in the various worlds of art and pop, and never lost either his wits or his footing. In short, he reminds me as do few others of what poets might be in a common world if only they could or would.

—Robert Creeley

These obit-elegies are among the best poems in the canons of contemporary world literature. They bring the reader up close and personal into the persons and places of Gerard Malanga's unique and life-long creative visionary gift. They are wonderful portraits of those many great talents he knew and/or respected (or not) including himself. A true poet.

—Charles Plymell

As he rounds the corner of his seventies, Gerard Malanga's new poems are steeped in a past that is intricately present. Figures and scenes from his overlapping lives—poet, photographer, dancer, man-about-town—press on him, and bring along the light in the room, the street, the trees, and any questions that remain. It's all one poem, a kind of architecture of memory, as past and present commingle to "whisper sweet nothings," the moving song of a pivotal cross-cultural figure.

—Aram Saroyan

Sometimes you dream that there's someone you love who loves you... you wake up & for a few minutes you know that somewhere there's someone you love who loves you... & then you wake up into being awake. Gerard's poems are like that...

—Peter Lamborn Wilson

The New Mélancholia & Other Poems

Also by Gerard Malanga

Screen Tests: A Diary (with Andy Warhol) (1967)
The Last Benedetta Poems (1969)
10 Poems for 10 Poets (1970)
chic death (1971)
Incarnations: Poems 1965-1971 (1974)
Ten Years After: The Selected Benedetta Poems (1977)
This Will Kill That (1983)
Three Diamonds (1991)
Mythologies of the Heart (1996)
No Respect: New & Selected Poems 1964-2000 (2001)
AM: Archives Malanga, Volumes 1, 2, 3, & 4 (2011)
Malanga Chasing Vallejo: Selected Poems, César Vallejo (2014)
Tomboy & Other Tales (2014)
In Remembrance of Things Past, The Autobiography of Gerard Malanga
(2015, wch remains unpublished)
Whisper Sweet Nothings & Other Poems (2017)
Cool & Other Poems (2019)

Gerard Malanga

The New Mélancholia & Other Poems

Bottle of Smoke Press
New York

The New Mélancholia & Other Poems © 2021 by Gerard Malanga

Grateful acknowledgment is made to the following publications in which some of these poems first appeared: ***Art & Letters*** for Gavin Maxwell, poet & naturalist, 1914-1969, Tom Raworth, poet, 1938-2017; ***Love Love 2*** (Paris) for Anna Karina, movie star, 1940-2019, London Photo 2016, and Self-Portrait après the 3rd Avenue El; ***Love Love 3*** (Paris) for April 11th 2019, Brief Encounter, and Mélancholia 2; ***Maintenant 14*** (2020) for Romain Gary, novelist, 1914-1980; ***Poetry*** (May 2020) for 6:22 a.m. and Virginia Woolf, July 1902.

The poem, April 11th 2019, was read by Gerard Malanga in a taped recording on August 9, 2020 for 1 Future/Global Monday Blues (Johannesburg, South Africa) in partnership with CHK 12 and Hare Mame.

Thanking the editors for their full support of my work.

Chiswick trees, Chiswick, London, November 24th 2019
Cover contactsheet © by Gerard Malanga

ISBN: 978-1-937073-96-1 (Paperback)
             978-1-937073-97-8 (Hard Cover)

Bottle of Smoke Press
29 Sugar Hill Road
North Salem, NY 10560

bospress.net

Contents

Section III: Stories   63

Section IV: Dreaming from 4 to 6 in the morning.   75

Section V: A genuine epiphany — **111**

Section VI: The New Mélancholia — **115**

for N. B.

2nd time around

A-wop-bop-a-loo-bop-a-wop-bam-boom!   *Little Richard*

We do not want your civilization.   *Crazy Horse*

One does not have one heart for Man and one for animals.
One has a heart or one does not.   *Alphonse de Lamartine*

...the muse is not to be won by the sacrifice of time,
and time I have not to spare.   *William Wordsworth*

At the heart of all great art is an essential melancholy.
    Federico García Lorca

For nothing in the world is it worth turning one's back
on what one loves.   *Albert Camus*

...memory nourishes the heart...   *Marcel Proust*

The ultimate object of all Poetry is Truth.   *Edgar Allan Poe*

The final wish is love.   *Allen Ginsberg*

The imagination sets us free to merge with memory and take off
as we like, flying straight on until morning. Just like Peter Pan said.
    patti smith

Perhaps the measure of the best art is that it does not excite envy.
    Norman Mailer

...When you live too long you end up knowing nobody.   *Romain Gary*

I

Growing up in The Bronx

le vite nuove

     It's apparent I've been busy with my own *vite nuove* from day one,
attempting to recount the history of my times,
as if in saying so,
someone I once knew manages to cross the Ponte Vecchio
with an aura demarcating time. A slight, remembered voice,
a glowing state of grace,
en route to where, I wonder?
Piazza del Popolo?
Metropolitan Ave?
the Saint-Germain-des-Près?
The Coney Island Steeplechase of fun & mirrors.
The *Playland* of Times Square where Gerardo took me after suppers
       at the Horn & Hardart Automat.
I wonder why we never posed inside the photobooth
father/son look-alikes huddled in together smiling, laughing.
Our faces flush with fun.
And then the late nite rush the D train to The Bronx,
walking past the cottage where a man named Edgar Allan Poe
once lived surrounded by the silky drifts of snow
and howling winds. I sometimes thought to visit him. I didn't know.
I never thought someday *the moving finger writes and having writ,*
my pen moves on just like his. Each window candle-lit.
Those names addresses disconnected phones.
Those yesteryears. No way of reaching back.
You find yourself alone
say settled under some idyllic English tree
without *emotions recollected in tranquility...*

without recollections...

...without tranquility.

Gerard Malanga dies.

Every poem is a throw of the dice in weather fair or foul.
What will this morning hold in store?
Will I top the last one? I don't know. It's chancy.
Certain stories almost lost to history
till I find myself diving into the unconscious and beyond.
The segue into tight cinematographies,
into voice-overs echoing, conversations, bit by bit.
Stéphane Mallarmé aka Étienne long since gone.
He's not the only one to finally reach an obscured passing, a railroad siding.
I am my only guide now.
What you see and hear is someone else standing in for me,
except I'm not standing up. I'm sitting down!
And in all that time the writing's never stopped,
though frozen in my steps, but not so with the words, the many sounds.
They speak, the music answers. I must sing
a lovely tune or dance
the many kinds of "swing,"
the many niche come alive in my breast pocket.
I've tap-danced through the waves of time.
I've beach-bummed many beaches. Homeless, penniless, garrulous.
Many a romance started on these sands.
The faces I recall vividly, but somewhere soon, maybe not so vividly.
Memory has its patience & regrets.
As fate would have it, something always gives.
The rabbit hole is waiting for my plunge.
Someone dies in 1995 or '96. Do I recall? Am I supposed to?
Am I preparing for another life? A return to life?
Still so many names, so many anecdotes.
It's been an odyssey as I journey on and on,
as landscapes rush me by outside this panoramic window
from Glasgow down to Central London, to the south of France.
It's raining a light rain now.
Why and where am I?
Will I ever find my way home to The Bronx?

curiosités

How can I say goodbye to something I'd never felt? Really, now!
Is it *Bonjour Tristesse* or *Adieu Tristesse?*
Either way,
it was never that for me
back in '58
when suddenly this phrase entered my invisible *lexique*
already bypassed in my adolescence as a happy child.
Why disrupt this urge remaining even happier in my curiosities?
I already knew my way around
in the lurky subways
and in those snarling traffics up above.
The haberdasheries that drew my eyes.
The hobby shoppes: the postage stamp collectibles,
the miniature HO gauge train sets.
Those travel agencies with their steamship postcard give-aways.
The world of tomorrow very much of the moment is not much of the moment now
when on any given day the sun's rays
break through fists of *plein-air* clouds as a guiding light from God.
Never a Hello, sadness for me!
Even the dark forests of my dreams would slink away among the mists
wherever I was heading,
                    heading now in my shaky curiosities,
as the D train rocked me back to The Bronx.

The MacArthur

In quoting Whitman, *"...I haven't gain'd the acceptance*
of my own time...",
or as Burroughs, Bill once told me,
"You have the mark about you",
...then what's my time, I wonder.
Should these loquacities persist,
will poetry not survive posterity?
If being so,
so be it so.
So be it that my ghost still lingers
once explored amongst the Highland brooks & creeks,
the streams meandering,
netting butterflies,
or simply daydreaming,
or the call to lunch Emma had prepared,
a salami Swiss cheese on a hard roll.
My favorite soda pop, Hoffman's root beer.
My dad Jerry soaking up a tan amongst the apple trees
high on a hill across the Pancake Hollow Road.
Such silences surrounding
with little else distracting him,
a lone buzzing bumble bee.
He was my chaperon.
He'd sewn my clothes.
A new suit or a sporty autumn coat.
I'd just turned four.
He had a rhythm all his own.
The arm lifting.
His hand gentle, lifting.
"Here, try it on," he'd say.
My cause célèbre
unforeseen nor for the struggles I'd endure
outside the soul within me decades later.
Never mind!
I've won the jackpot in my sleep,
and nothing less a hundred years hence can fully answer
how I picked my battles and won the war.

Self-portrait après the 3rd Avenue El

Dear me,
        I was a documentarian before I became a photographer.
Don't ask me why? It might've been my insatiable curiosity
for barely-looked-at unsuspecting details.
The worn wainscoting,
the moistened, rusticated blocks,
the angled light squeezed through the sleepers from above.
What do you expect from a 12-year-old? What are the risks?
A stray tuxedo cat left hungry in the street.
The first foto I snapped contained no people.
Just lots of shadows, this & that.
Just the silence of a Sunday early afternoon
as my dad looked on, and then away, and back again.
He wondered what was I doing with my brand-new camera.
He wondered why the street was empty.
He stood a ways away and let me do my thing.
What was my thing?
The ability to point & shoot and then move on?
A shop window reflected with the Brownie Hawkeye dangling from my neck
amid all this deconstruction & debris,
ghostly remnants soon to be.
These silent tracks ending in a precipice of time as I looked up.

The Harlem River Terminal in The Bronx
for the New York, Westchester & Boston Railway.

You remain haunted for as long as I can remember,
even through my adolescence,
my grown-up years.
A building can do that to you sometimes,
as I might've read somewhere,
but *where* I don't recall.
There you were solitary, seemingly empty 4 storeys tall,
across from the handball courts,
with not a hint of your former afterglow.
How was I to know?
And yet something something
about you wanted me to know with each passing:
the months
the days
the years
every time I passed on that gentle graded slope
of Willis Ave,
with you emerging in your cloistered silence
beckoning my eyes,
living through the seasons,
those sudden sweeping downpours,
those silent sleets.
You deserved more for an orphan like yourself...

Mrs. Gurney...

        In what we remember & what we've forgotten,
one instance deletes the other,
until the shards of memories, the remnants
remaining, only to confuse,
the après & befores.
My childhood in The Bronx filled with curiosities.
Mrs. Gurney... or was it Guernsey?
You were of German descent
I recall with no accent.
You lived in a one-bedroom flat on the ground-floor,
off to the left as you step into the hallway from the vestibule,
from light to darker.
I'd come down to visit you on occasion. Don't you remember?
I must've been no more than 8.
You welcomed me in. Cookies & milk.
You opened your honeymoon album. You were a widow now
to what remains documented in the fotos laid bare,
mostly taken in the southwest. Arizona. Why would I remember that?
Or I could be way off. What's the luck?
There was one shot that appeared more than once as I turned the folios over.
A tree silhouetted as an ostrich against a bleached-out sky,
furled or unfurled. I can't tell wch, even now.
You made a point of calling it the "ostrich tree,"
but we didn't know the species...
and then one dog-day afternoon as I passed your door I sensed you were gone.
Does this tree still exist, I would wonder.
Does time hold fast or let go?
What's lost to memory?
Words are the only claimant to remembering, but that won't do.
7 decades now, I'm no further nor nearer. I've not a clue.

Ethel Waters w/ Carl Van Vechten's self-portrait

Already at 16, I could distinguish between the generic
　　　　　　　　black & white portraitures
and a Carl Van Vechten print.
The first foto I laid eyes on was a self-portrait
wch included Ethel Waters
up against these flourishes of palm trees moonbeams lightning bolts.
She was the best.
She was always "in character."
She could easily be your friend.
She could talk to Mr. Bluebird on your shoulder.
Surely, as I knew her then, I know her now
beyond those disappearing histories.
The street talk
& the shop talk
& the sweet talk.
Those street kids skipping rope or tossing jacks.
Those blacks & whites of East Harlem where my mom grew up.
"Little Italy" to some.
3rd Avenue with its elevated ghosts
resisting memories.

1983

That was the year Jerry my dad passed on.
He died where he lived
a dozen or so years in Zephyrhills, FLA
in a ramshackle 3-room flat with a screened-in porch
wch I'm certain he never looked out of,
except for those cool September breezes,
those changing angled arcings of the sun & moon,
the chipmunks & the crickets & the pixies to keep him company.
For it seems he lived forever alone, forever still.
He rarely read or watched TV. No pets.
I didn't see one when I visited in '72,
the year I saw *The Godfather*
at a local cinema in downtown Houston,
and the year I saw Jerry last alive.
He'd shrunken in size.
I found myself looking down at him as he looked up at me.
I had no such recollection in my adolescence.
I was still the runt at 12, even with the camera 'round my neck.
I was still curious
& loved looking at fotos in the magazines,
New York's Changing Scene
in the Sunday *Coloroto* of the Daily News.
The movie ads I'd clip 'n save into blank scrapbooks,
and then the movies themselves,
Carol Reed's *The Man Between*, before being knighted.
Visconti's *The Leopard*. He already held sway through family lineage.
I'd gone back to see them more than once
when they reached the Valentine
on Fordham Road when Fordham still had its wrought-iron lampposts.
The trolley tracks long paved over. The cobblestones, too.
It was a hope against hope for their return,
and then my imagination faded in & faded out. I dreamt elsewhere.
New York was changing fast & I was changing fast,
caught up in my own little world,
what few years left remaining
before discovering this thing called poetry
keeping me forever enthralled.
The words carrying me aloft on angel wings.
The dreams in increments of time.
Some nites were dreamless. Others not and still others
filled with swirling dances, strange intrigues
with people I seemed to recognize but never knew in real life.
I can't remember when Jerry paid me a visit in my sleep,
or if he ever will.
        I wake into my wakefulness, into the *absolue*.

Carmela Rocco

My grandmother, Carmela, my mother's mother, died before I was five.
I think I must've been three, at the very least,
because I have this vague recollection
that the year was sometime in 1945, but no later.
Her departure didn't stun me.
She meant nothing to me,
because I have no exact memory of her,
no rccollections except for the one visit at her tiny apartment
on Bainbridge Ave before reaching Fordham Road to the south.
And yet I couldn't understand what had happened,
and therefore was left with no dream of her.
The one of two existing photos I have of her
when she must've been in her early seventies
looks a lot like how my mom Emma
would look in her old age.
They bore a striking resemblance to each other, the same smile,
but like some long lost silent movie,
there is no voice, not even how she sounded, even.
It's a reality easy to accept,
because in the end
it meant nothing to me.
I don't even remember my mom grieving,
and that was the end of it.
And yet she had a separate life from mine, my grandmother.
It was unwise to meditate about this.
And so I feel no anticipated regret,
nor for the very last flickers of a consciousness,
nor for an after-life, like a bluebird flying in one window
and out the other,
              we flutter after a moment in the after-light.

Edgar Allan Poe

   Even Edgar Poe seems to wanna keep you secret metaphorically.
So for now, you still remain the "you"
as the archetype traverses centuries & those endless desert shores.
"Nameless *here* for evermore."*
You've had your muses
as I've had mine.
How would you know? Edgar, you had to know,
seeing into a future dimly lit, trying to compare the nitty-gritty.
No way to penetrate the past.
Einstein has a lock on Time.
There were no subways then where you were living up in Fordham
in what would later be The Bronx,
less than 3 blocks where I was growing up. My adolescence,
my teenage years without the sophistication
who you were and what you mean to me.
Not even I could perceive those futures all the more to know.
Those *Lenores* who went by other names
not even coming close. The living Loulou fame.
The différence between the fictive & those real realities.
The D train of the IND Line that would take me far
and open up horizons to the unexpected
while you lingered for a year or two
braving winter storms, the biting cold,
the onset of a pneumonia, a consumptive bout, even.
Your imagination more isolated than those *evermores*.
It was fated that we'd cross paths as I was turning 5
when stopping at your doorstep
my dad snapped the picture in all my innocence.
And so yours was the first name in my vocabulary,
and still I'd have no idea or any way to place you in a context
till I grew into one some years later,
as if blessed by a make-believe wholly unanticipated
and yet made more real as well.

*The Raven

Dr. Walter Benjamin redux

Walter Benjamin, professeur.
                    Up until 1940 with your "childlike modes of acquisition..."
then all went dark... so I'm on my own.
I look around in awe.
Will I recall more so than before?
Will I forget the "cutting out of figures..." you so describe so well?
The scrapbooks piling up, the pulp sheets firm to my touch
and then one day my dad stored them all
in Uncle Willy's garage
3 blocks north
and my curiosities wandered further on,
turning pages from last week's tabloids
to marvel at the fashion spreads.
But did I really know what I'd been looking at, Walt...
a future unforetold?
Did I really know my way around the subways?
Those darknesses *souterrain*.
Never to be 12 again.
Never to walk amongst those shopping sprees along the Fordham Road
as the 3 p.m. dog-day light descends,
to lift the camera hanging round my neck.
Those dimestore windows reflecting back the drizzled rain.
The local record shoppes, the clothing
I shopped for on the sneak.
The houndstooth jacket w/ its peak
lapels I must've worn to death.
The McCreedy-Schreiber shoes custom-made to fit my feet, my falling arches.
The tartar-plaid poncho--did I
outgrow it? Where did it go?
Documented up until c. '62 in snapshots, then no more.
The names I'd seen. I was good at names. Too many names.
Curiosities emerging from the darkness of the night before.
The neighborhood has changed.
Where has the low-slung building at the corner
gone? What's not the same?
Where am I wandering...
so... so far distant now. "Truth's transmissibility"
stayed with me since, stays with me now.
What lies behind the gloss,
                    the dénouement?

Bronx Adventure

      What will happen when I die? Will I have lived a full & robust life
with lifelong friends?
One of my fondest memories was photographing Edgar Allan Poe's white
                                                clapboard cottage
with my Brownie-Hawkeye,
tilting the camera like some crazy little kid,
waiting for Mr. Poe to suddenly appear
and asking what's that I'm holding in my hand!
In interviews, I've been asked, What's it like growing up in The Bronx,
like it were some kind of foreign entity,
some distant kingdom uninhabited, ringed by steep & sweeping cliffs.
I was too young to know its obscure Dutch & Swedish legacies,
its ghostliness, its many picture shows
where I'd while the time away
with foreign flicks like *The Lovers, The Leopard,*
Wild Strawberries where I'd find myself running through a field of hide & seek.
Those drizzling rainy streets,
those cobblestones that marked the way to yet another way.
The woods that bordered on my aunt & uncle's house in Pelham Bay.
The trolleys that would take me home some ungodly hour.
I was filled with wonder.
                          Why do I feel this way?

After winter, spring...

After winter, spring.... Life can't make up its melancholic mind.
Dear Dad, Jerry, I've come to visit you in nowhere Florida.
How are you? You OK? You still have all your hair! A greyish white.
You're 75 now. I rub your head. We sort of smile.
The Bronx is still The Bronx. The slow fade is frozen now...
                         so are the sprocket holes.
Nicola, you can't see me. I see you I see you in that last slow moment
crossing the Tavern on the Green parking lot--
you didn't know that that was that--to where
it is you're going.
An almost sandy hue surrounding you....
Sasha, my grey chartreux,
you were named after Alexander Hammid,
husband to Maya Deren.
You were a gentle, quiet soul. Inspiring.
As I was leaving, your care-giver called me back.
A 2nd goodbye you waved on to me,
shared through each other's eyes.
A moment of moments, the last.
                         And I felt blessed.
My life is filled with many blessed moments, many minutes,
a few lasting seconds, even. A passing glance.
A *coup de foudre*, as they say in ancien France.
That flash of lightning going nowhere, sometimes somewhere.
These are my "Roots of Heaven."
A history of silences, absences unwritten or unnamed.
A nite filled with unrelenting rain & dreams says it all or not at all.
This morning I feed you all, Sasha, Zazie, Xena. I take my bow.
I take my pills.
I pull on my stretch socks.
I glance over at a poem gone nowhere from the nite before.
Life is circular, circuitous, a guessing game.
I go on with my day, all the same.
It could happen anywhere, a sudden pain,
a sudden flashing darkness,
then a dark cloud riffling over.
No time goodbyes to all that. The memories remain.
                         Those moments the beneficiaries of truth.

I remember things through photographs…

      I remember things through photographs… dates, names, even anecdotes.
Those hilly empty lots,
those pointed paving stones,
those subway rides going somewhere. Where?
My father's face reflected in the wired glass.
What I recall, I forget.
I began taking photographs just before my 12th birthday.
The little plastic Kodak Brownie snug in my hands.
How do I know this?
Many times I've touched my soul.
I've touched those darknesses,
those street facades.
Edgar Poe's white clapboard cottage in The Bronx.
The iron-wrought lampposts while looking up,
backlit by naked gloomy skies.
What memories are sustainable,
what not.
Those white cottages as far away as Cornwall's ghostly coast.
The El tracks angled from above.
Sunlight pouring through the sleepers.
Memories sometimes confusing,
                      the lights & darks.

My very 1st photograph, c. 1950...

In a photograph, everything begins to look like everything else
when I raised the two-and-a-quarter box camera
in looking down into the tiny glass,
framing the shot of my aunt & uncle's house
at the end of Tiemann Ave
to catch a memory
of a house no longer standing.
How many houses would claim an exacting fate?
How many times
time would stay frozen at the sounding of a click, barely audible
in those days before the reflex mirror shuttered?
Aunt Dolly & Uncle Joe were myths defying time
by their transatlantic sailing in 1955 late summer.
Would The Bronx forever be the same?
Would my memories of them persist or simply change, half-forgotten?
On the day of my 1st Holy Communion
I stand straight as a young soldier
in their backyard, a garden really, a fountain nearly dead-center behind me
and the glory of black & white
hand-tinted into color,
transforming the mundane into artsy kitsch...
& I am affixed
forever in a time long since past, collecting dust in a shoebox.
Was it a Thom McAn or a Florsheim?
Or a pair of orthopaedic high-tops lined so,
my falling arches would soon rise to normal.
I was of an age to remember.
I was of an age where everything begins looking differently,
forgetful of the past as from a future unbeknownst to me,
that being left-handed I begin seeing with my left eye also.
My 1st photograph was defined by the act of looking & looking & looking...
It must've been the last house on the block left standing,
left empty, then empty still.
Trusting in my instincts has no regrets.
What I was trying to save was to remember through a perforated snapshot,
beyond the darkened woods,
the rising flocks in silhouette in unison,
                                        the murmured breezes.

Cousin, Marianna

There were no city lights at dusk where she was growing up.
Tiemann Ave was an absolutely quiet street
just off the Pelham Parkway
where no trolleys were allowed to go, it seemed.
Marianna, my 1st cousin, so far & distant, with her chubby looks.
The lasting recognition amongst the few fotos
left remaining, still unsorted.
She had to be at least 10, maybe 12 years or older than me.
I have no way of knowing. We never played together.
Those visits on the edge of an unspoken loneliness.
Left alone in the living-room, all I did was look
& look around, as if I were a camera.
Even the upholstered furnishings seemed to be receding.
I never knew her interests.
Where did she go to school,
what movies did she see,
where did she shop for clothes?
She had her formal portrait taken once
at the Delma Studios, East Fordham Road, but no date given.
It seemed my world gravitated to the backyard garden.
I was my own best company when it came to nature.
Several snapshots survive.
My 1st Holy Communion amongst them, hand-tinted.
I am trapped to know more & more.
She sailed with her parents, my Aunt Dolly Uncle Joe,
her future husband Arthur,
on the ill-fated Andrea Doria a year before its sinking.
Those few remaining moments above-deck would be our last.
A harbor breeze taking hold.
Just the one color snap Emma took.
Now all a blur.
There never were any photo opportunities.
Our lives were just too casual.
The rest is memory.
The long-term memory growing shorter shorter
                                                    I'm unable to recall.

March 9th 2020

Dad dear Dad,
             It's not everyday, your birthday, that I get the chance
wishing you a bright Hello.
Your years numbering 1-2-3,
as one thing or another occupies my mythic time,
like rinsing the dishes,
changing the kitty-litter, napping with the cats,
or formatting my latest poem on Instagram.
It's not everyday I meander back some other time now long forgotten.
The walks we've made along that dreary stretch of Webster Ave
known for nothing, past the *Decatur,*
with its marquee neon blown out rusted, now forever lost.
It was a hike,
but we made it.
A favorite park bench in the Botanic Gardens
where I played make-believe
up & down this obscure knoll
losing all sense of pre-existing time & somewhat winded
while you glanced off into leafy space & then your watch.
Dad, I don't know where my poems are coming from,
                                   but then I never knew.

Gerardo Malanga, tailor, dry goods salesman, 1897-1983

Dear Dad, dear Jerry,
                          I can't find what to say irksome.
There never was a time
making the connections felt & understood.
Always an unspoken closeness.
Always my life rooted in words & yours of silences.
The close readings of Marcel Proust,
if I can still wade through the Post-Its,
or to ask about your troubles.
What about the high shoes I was wearing for how long?
You supported my curiosity
that led from one montage to the next
when in my nightly dreams
the world worked wonders those few seconds inbetween,
those endless lifetimes, those likenesses
catching up
& moving on.
The sprocket holes as residue.
And I am clueless
as to who is whom
in the family fotos,
even though I can place the backgrounds,
the very neighborhoods we visited.
I got the hang of it.
Those times are precious.
We never posed together in the photobooth.
In my memory, we did.
The Bronx Botanical Gardens & the Children's Zoo
après Arthur Ave food shopping
après Allen Street & Orchard Street
après St James Park, Poe Park. I was King of the Hill.
For a moment we stand still staring out
at the lonesome skyscrapers across the Upper Bay.
The angel with the torch behind us pointing heavenward.
Jerry holding my hand. I feel safe.
                                  I'd just turned 4.

Gerard Malanga, 1943 to the present.

It's only *after* that they remember you. Total strangers, mind you!
They remember you for what they've read. He lived *the life!*
They remember your ghost even as a clue to the *existentiel.*
They remember only your shadow in passing;
your elongated silhouette across the paving-stones
at 5:00 p.m. a summer's day somewhere the East Village,
The Bronx, where have you.
St.-Germain de Prés the VIe 1970.
Loulou waiting at the *Flore*, all-smiles. The drifting off...
and then everything goes ghostly. The snowy twilight settling in.
Years of wanderings, homelessness, house-sittings,
the Sloppy Joe's, and still the poems keep coming.
Round-the-world in one delirious direction only,
as in a dream somewhere the rambla, the arroyo,
and still the poems keep coming strong.
This morning everything seemed a bit blurry.
I need to reach for my reading glasses, *oi, vai!*
but they're left outside the dream... and I'm inside!
No way can I reach through without crashing the unconscious.
The choice do I sleep or do I wake? I wake!
Now all else is in the past. The sleep. The dream.
Mallarmé is in the past by candlelight and really drifting off!
Shelley is in the past remaining imageless *before photography;*
before the mirror-image. Way before.
Names and names and more names become a scrambled mess.
I wanna reach out. The looking-glass reflects back
the one side only; not the other. The dark side. The *existentiel.*
The 1920s. Paris. No!
The late 60s. Milan. Rome. Yes! No!
Cities of the night.
Cities in the rain.
The names remaining & so much more.
Has it all been make-believe, *after all?* I wanna know.
Has life been blessed?
The many friends. The many lovers. Some gone to rest.
Names criss-crossed and star-crossed.
The drifting off. Even the pre-posthumous, the gossipy.
All's well that ends well... or does it end?
Tell me the time. What time is it? I wanna know.

Antonette Martone, 1909-2011

Dearest Betty,
              Who are you to me? Even now I ask.
Last time I saw you was at my mom's wake in Brooklyn 1997, May 6th
& few words if any were exchanged & then you left.
I have vivid memories
& memories not so vivid a disconnect
visiting you your sister Cora
in the Kingsbridge section of The Bronx
& I couldn't have been no more than 5 or 6
because we'd catch the trolley
from the Fordham section
wch took an hour
till the line was ripped up in 1949
& then we'd take the bus
with that steep incline I loved so much
& the visits were most festive, as I recall,
& you'd shown such kindnesses to me.
No one told me
could it be
we were 1st or 2nd cousins even?
Was Carlo Malanga your dad or granddad?
He was the oldest of my dad's brothers by 20 years, zio Carluce.
He was present when Jerry & Emma visited with you
on their wedding day in 1942, May 2nd, to be exact,
because he was standing tall in a surviving snapshot
you must've snapped
with Jerry's camera,
remaining to this day this mystery
till cousin Gloria filled in the gaps
& here my words become fuzzy fuzzier
till I'm left in the dark searching for the light
& for the names & for those "memories,"
as Marcel Proust once said, "nourishing the heart."

II

"The Lives They Lived"

Tom Raworth, poet, 1938-2017

Tom,
    I wanna say to you like what
your namesake Thomas Hardy once conveyed,
that "Time changes everything except something within us..."
and it isn't just the poetry, per se,
the time we talked nonsense
'cross the men's urinal at Bard College
before your reading debut
and all you could do
was commiserate your travails
so so confused
at the ER in nearby Rhinebeck that afternoon.
What a way to spend the day!
Had it always been that way with you
spiralling downwards inside the dust & gloom?
I can't remember the year. 2007 or so? That sounds right.
And now I'm several months too late
in catching up with you in the former U.K.
to do lunch, snap a snapshot or two,
some wayside tavern in the windy Cornwalls,
the nestling curlews plovers chorussing here & there.
Your quick noonday darkness in those distant corners, rocky shores
where lurk a few unfinished poems,
the bits & pieces of a life yet to be relived.
Your spirit ranging on and on.
I reckon it's like slipping into sleep, a darker sleep,
when you've pretty much winded out
and waking somewhere else
to find a summer's day
with scents of new mown hay
coming in your window.
After you'd gone, the autumn descended on my dog-day memories.

Cecil Taylor, jazz composer, 1929-2018.

Hey Cecil!

       Whence the unconscious?

I doubt even you expected those unruly hours to go frozen suddenly

with the shades drawn,

              or to shout to high heavens, "What happened?!"

Life just stopt. Whatcha expect?

What was it you wanna say to me?

Why me? I hold no magic secrets, no oily elixir that would do its magic,

its elusive magic 'cross those striding keys.

You remained stubborn, uncompromising, unflattering.

Well, that's not exactly true.

You could be easily coaxed.

You could be walkin down the street in a drizzle when a rhythm gets ya

and you keep it going in your head,

You've got rhythm...

until you find a darkend doorway where to jot it down,

da doom da doom da doom.

Where from there would ya go? Is there life after life?

Don't let it slip,

and then you slip into some unexpected rabbit hole,

a plunge into existence,

and suddenly a rabbit greets you.

"Br'er rabbit is my name!"

That so?

Death is like that. Just a talkin rabbit.

One syllable and then you're past that.

Then you're unreachable, a million miles from nowhere.

Then you're back walkin in the rain.

Giuseppe Maria Scotese, Italian filmmaker, 1916-2002.

There are several inroads I could clear within this poem filling in the gaps.
Several openings as I foresaw
would lead me to an end without an end,
like in the ending of a movie where the title zooms in suddenly,
the sound turned off.
An Antonioni trick I've much admired and mimicked once,
like in an ending to end all ends,
I would make up for what's surely absent, lost.
The one encounter we had in 1966 New York
when you said, "I want to cast you in my movie."
Cast me?!
Che cosa movie?
        As memories go,
there's one slow dissolving fade on a dirty snowy street.
What brought you to New York from Rome?
Why did we meet?
What happened in the intervening years?
Did you fulfill those elusive goals?
Were there tragedies crowding out your memories?
Our fated paths no longer fated, never crossed again. *Perché?*
No one would believe this!
You spoke gently of your daydreams,
camera set-ups, continuities. You recounted
all those stories foretold & unforetold
as you go along waiting for the next camera angle,
the dolly run-thru,
                to continue where we left off.

Gavin Maxwell, poet & naturalist, 1914-1969

Gavin,
      I often wonder why you wore dark glasses in your seaside cottage,
away from windows, from autumn drafts.
A lemur attacking you from behind in your London flat,
scarring your eyes and nearly blinding you.
What the fuck were you thinking?!--that you
could calm its wildness, calm its charm
from swinging tree to tree?
I prayed for your recovery as I turned the page.
I clutched my chest.
Love knows no bounds for the wildness in all God's earthly creatures.
Surely, the otters were your friends. They're like pussy cats.
They are trusting. I've seen your photographs.
It's been decades now.
No sign of otters at your doorstep,
on your sofa, sound asleep, rolling on your bed.
No sign even of your shadow stretched across those snowy Scottish winters.

Nicolas Roeg, film director, 1928-2018

Nic,
    You had this ability to record the world as is.
A moment when a "moving photograph" comes out of nowhere suddenly,
or when a flock of Monarch butterflies came sweeping through
                                 your leaded window.
You didn't say a word.
You closed the script, face down.
The late autumn light angling in just so.
Those neglected moments
or the spare room of a country house
somewheres on England's southern coast.
What's to come and what's now gone.
Lost in the distant woods one sunlit afternoon,
you stare entranced.
                 The storyboards imagined.

Richard Wright, novelist, 1908-1960

Dear Richard Wright,
      We were fated never to meet, even through mentor-friends, Willard & Marie.
A street corner midtown Manhattan lunch-time,
the New York Public Library Reading Room in the lamplight glow.
Not even the boardwalk out at Coney Island.
A subway ride where I mistook you for someone else across the aisle.
Who is this someone else I've long forgotten,
or in any other wakened dream
where the residues last & last in the frozen fadings.
You were 5 years gone when I arrived in Paris '65.
No way to leap-frog time.
You led other kinds of lives.
You wrote & wrote in those damp stilled mornings still remaining,
but in no way could I catch up with you.
Your life beyond mine by years & years. Now, even more so.

Ingeborg Bachmann, Austrian poet, 1926-1973

Dear Ingeborg,
              I've been meaning to conjure you for several years.
But *why* now?
It would be late in '67, early '68, no '67,
that we crossed paths,
ristorante Bolognese through Elsa Morante's kindness
and nothing much transpired.
My mind still forms a blank like a sieve.
I don't believe you spoke a word of English,
otherwise we surely would've spoken,
exchange ideas, maybe
even a poem or two recited to each other.
You wore a gray flannel suit, I seem to recall,
though not worth recalling. Your hair a dirty blonde
cropped short just below the ears,
but it's your smile of curiosity what got me,
because you smiled directly at me. Could that be right?
What's there to say, if anything?
What, what could be said?
Those words, those precious sentences gone missing,
still missing, unrecollected.
You're like some sort of ghost.
A series of like movie-stills of the mind,
bruised in the corners, the emulsion cracked,
as with all such ephemera.
Time has forgotten how little I recall,
adding up so much more suddenly.
The blacks & whites unspooling,
              and now time is missing, stuck in reverse.

Maurice Utrillo, Paris painter, 1883-1955

Maurice,
          You appeared to be a kindly man, a happy man, in the few fotos I remember
strolling with your English cocker spaniels
on your country grounds, Le Vésinet,
when you weren't at the easel.
You didn't paint *en plein air,* but from memory.
Photos don't... or I taught myself that photographs don't lie,
but memories have been known to be deceptive.
Yeah, memory has a bad rap.
The mind plays tricks on the mind,
but for you every brushstroke is a stroke of memory.
Every street a street you followed & remembered.
The few brushed-in figures appear walking away from you,
as if their backs were to the camera,
but there is no camera.
Just your eye guided by the hand.
The naked eye of far-reaching memory & memories.
No stories to be shared, or so it seems.
Why did they stand still or walk away from you?
You were a kindly man. Then why?
The houses mostly shuttered to the naked eye,
as if all life were shuttered,
and yet and yet you were never lonely in your quiet walks.
You went your way. Turned corners mostly.
It's autumn. Winter now.
Your eyes remember.
                    You are not deceived.

Peter Orlovsky, poet, 1933-2010.

Peter buddy,
        You & I were friends more so than Allen.
We'd joke a lot.
We got beyond the poetry & circled round.
Anne Buchanan aka Anne Plymell
was your girl and then mine. Don't ask me why.
We traded off the way we'd be trading poems. A joint or two.
She became a subtext to a further history beyond mine
and then was lost. Just dropped off the planet.
Or the way we shared food,
shopping the moms-&-pops, as casual as that.
The Lower East Side
still the Lower East Side, gloomy in some respects.
And then when would we ever find the time to write?
We were too busy laughing, too busy living.
Parting ways also became a pastime to a history
we were so much a part of
we didn't pay much attention to,
like a pot of mint tea or stirring a chicken broth.
It was like we were inside each other's writing for a while.
Nothing was ever fated between us to continue,
even when we'd take a breather, now & then
we'd be passing through that seedy grungy Tompkins Square
on our way to somewhere else. Not a care
in the world. Let's sit down a while and share a laugh.
You couldn't even spell right! Ha-ha.
I'm getting to be more like you now!
It's summer now. No, it's fall.
The leaves of grass remain unquoted.
A street I've since forgotten, that far east.
Someone's long lost address.
                A dream or two.

Anna Karina, movie star, 1940-2019

Anna sweetheart,
        How do I explain your death to others
when I can't even explain it to myself.
Simply, what you've done in your life will outlive you.
But these are not exactly the right words.
When I encountered you
in the movies,
you appeared to be everlasting.
Now with your passing
you are unchanging.
Your image fixed in a heavenly sphere of darks & lights.
What I do in the everyday
is what you might've done, too.
I go shopping for clothes at Le Bon Marché.
I might've run into you in the scarves dept. browsing,
or had I taken the Métro out to Les puces Clignancourt,
you might've been on the same train,
and I offered you my seat.
Would you have taken it? Maybe.
Who's to know in a universe
where variables outnumber those synchronous moments
where crossing bd. Saint-Germain,
you go one way while I go the other
in the walking rain,
where shopping for produce or for a bulk of black tea
is the norm if, in fact, we inhabit the same arrondissement.
Our lives are a series of *improvisations.*
Mornings when the same sun rises for us,
but our *réalité* might not cohere or imagine
what life will be like twenty years hence,
and now you're gone,
I cannot imagine kissing you behind the neck most mornings
like the way you did in the movies.
I cannot imagine you undressing at the edge of the bed,
cannot imagine us for *brunch* at the nearest parkside café,
for the dawn of a new day,
for day's end, for the gloom,
for the sudden rain-gust chasing us clear across Paris.
Your hair dripping wet,
your eyes soaked with those faux tears,
        your voice laughing & laughing & laughing.

Romain Gary, novelist, 1914-1980

Romain,
        I've missed the centennial of your birth by nearly 5 years.
Am I forgiven?
I've had you on my shelf for decades now.
My memory doesn't serve me right. Your *Roots of Heaven,*
a Hollywood spectacular,
yet I never saw it.
A movie much missed. Where was I
when it played the RKO Palace?
I was home alone in The Bronx, laid up with an earache. I was 15.
Your marriage to Jean Seberg,
remarkable for an unlikely duo... I take it back.
The perfecto you & you,
veiled in the imaginary.
You & Jean now legendary.
It's how to measure Time when time is all we have and staying happy.
Elusive to the touch, what's left?
Always the smart suit & tie, fitted to perfection in Oxford Street,
& vivid in the tabloid photographs.
I imagine much. *Imaginaire*
still takes me far & wide,
these separate *réalités,* separate still.
Those "spots of time," as Wordsworth marked them
in his nature wanderings.
To our lives before us, there are many.
Our parting words, there are few.
Our greetings passing through the Paris dusks in dream time,
we keep it loose, we keep it dreamy.
Your dreamy voice: "I had a lot of fun, thank you."
Your forever lasting, parting note.
A true gentleman & warrior.
                Adieu, adieu.

Bob Thompson, painter, 1937-1966

Dear Bob,
        You suddenly passed on when I was just a fledgling in 1966,
but now I've lost all sense of passing time,
and we'd barely had a word,
but the words linger,
your shaven face,
so unmistakable, the smiling warmth,
it all comes back,
but barely for a cinematic flashback.
Those jazzy nites in your oft-times crowded loft.
The music blasting.
The paper cups filling up the trash.
Those sun-bleached dawns crawling 'cross the Bouwerie.
The Jones Street diner light still on...
and life still going strong, and then you'd gone.
Why was it?
There must've been a reason, unlike the usual,
the "failing health" syndrome.
I'm sure you must've cared.
I looked for you a spell amongst all the detritus,
but you've been missed, obscured, lost, even.
Obscurité they say in French.
My words too, seem so obscured, to make them right,
so we'd connect. But where?
Time has a way of tricking time.
So does NYC.
So do the morning birds, the common sparrows,
and those other *curiosités,*
that's gotten us through the day.
Those nites, too, when the best in us surprises us,
                             still surprising us.

Cy Twombly, artist, 1928-2011

Cy,
    We were always on the peripheries, the périphérique,
both in life,
in Rome, in Paris earlier,
Hôtel La Louisiane,
                but you'd gone already.
I'd even misplaced your home address once,
and it's very easy
getting lost while wandering among Rome's ancient, newly fabricated paving stones,
or did I just imagine this
             5 decades since.
A sunlight misconstrued for some painted backdrop
warehoused at Cinecittà,
among the hammerings,
the distant echoings,
the erratic lunch-breaks,
or to the windblown, sandy Ostia, still off-season.
Even the sandwiches got sandy.
It's all coming back to me
and going back away, like some anachronistic scratchy fade-out,
that the poems touched on, no less.
Words chalked in, crossed out, illegible.
We never discussed Rilke & his Duino elegies.
It was always a Hello, Goodbye, ciao, and all the rest,
when added up don't add up to much
unless a sunset intervenes, a golden dusk, a disc,
white-washing everything. Suddenly
Giorgio Franchetti.
He'd shown me a great kindness without ever letting on.
All this distant now, those unrecollected memories.
I'd lost the thread
somewhere in the treeless outskirts, the EUR streets.
Everything gone silent, disarrayed.
It so happens.
            What was I looking for? Why & where?

Santu Mofokeng, apartheid photographer, 1956-2020

Howzit Santu,
        You & I have been kept *apart* & unawares of each other for far too long.
The stretch of ghostly sands
or the dark & dingy subways of New York
that would take us far & close in our imaginings
where we'd miss each other in the throngs,
the rushhour crush,
born in the photographs.
How heavy your darknesses, your angles gone askew.
How heavy was your camera bag?
I never bothered weighing mine. I'd say
5 lbs. of metal would've surely thrown my posture out,
that friends took notice I sometimes walked funny.
I have no way of asking you
the mundane
the obvious.
The "chase"
as often quoted by Bill Brandt, I recall.
His "shadows" & his "auras" carried over, impressed on you.
But I've lost the footnote amongst the crush of words, the harried emails.
Perhaps you kept a diary. I didn't.
A few times I misplaced some precious negatives, presumed them gone forever:
The Bowery Station before it was deformed, sacrilegious.
I found them in a box correctly labelled "Cats,"
so I never thought to look.
I knew I'd get a laugh outta you.
The old *adage* has it
when we search for one thing
we rediscover someone else. Nothing's lost. We speak the language.
Neither your time nor mine in New York's subways
                        where we glimpsed each other in the dark.

Bobby Driscoll, child star, 1937-1968

Bobby,
      You still out at Potter's Field Hart Island 6 feet under
Unmarked
Unidentified
Unwanted
?
having lost your way
among those Hollywood hills & extravaganzas.
You gave voice to the title role
in Walt Disney's *Peter Pan*
and every kid mimicked you. That cheery voice of yours, still yours
so unmistakable from down the block
calling out to me,
I'd throw the key out the window in a sock.
Vague recollections unlike
what's in the movies, not all make-believe.
If it's still in the mind, the secret outtakes, fragments,
then it's your roles making up for what's now lost:
Song of the South,
The Uncle Remus stories some say are racist, 1946.
Treasure Island with Robert Newton swaggering, even off the set.
Always a pint in his back pocket, you once told me.
And *The Window,* RKO,
wch I discovered on my own,
the best of the American film noir,
while perusing vintage posters at Jerry Ohlinger's movie shoppe.
Even in your presence,
there was something of the film noir in you, the darkened you
falling from those fames & starry lights
into a darkness tumbling further from afar.
So when we caught up
was an all-niter, w/ Dee Dee, your babe,
the acclaimed John Wieners, the poet,
even then consumed by his schizophrenic demons.
The 4 of us
way into the weee hours up on speed
at John's room in the Hotel Nassau,
a poor man's Chelsea,
up the block from Bloomingdale's.
And as that misty New York dawn that never sleeps,
we find ourselves shucked into the side street
where our riffs continue unabated
through your remaining days & months, though we didn't know.

Our histories shared to fill a trip book with greasy magic markings.
We'd smoke a fatty where O where I lost you,
my fellow Pisces,
           in the pre-dawn burnished hazy light.

Peter... Peter Beard

Dear Peter,
           You give me your Parisian movie star smile
for one everlasting, open moment,
as the golden hour
passes through you,
passes through some obscure window
in some obscure arrondissement
in some hidden penny thought
remaining hidden to this day
some nearly
40 years deep.
I'm on the subway on my way home
and you're suddenly in my consciousness.
How did I find myself here
like yesterday were yesterday
or the day before
in our shared enthusiasms,
in our love for God's heavenly
& earthly creatures
and so much more.
Rest easy in your dreams, dear friend,
as I do mine,
as I find myself running running running home
in a quickened pace...
and where is home
is where we've always been,
arriving one way,
then another.
It's been said I have a photographic memory
& it's been said here
yours is like the memory of an elephant,
an elephant that never forgets
                      never forgetting...

Denis Deegan, connoisseur of life, 1937-1994

Denis, dear Denis,
                There's so very little of anything regarding you
I hear myself repeating
like in a mantra
rising from the mists,
the salient stones,
the arboretum
with their hedged-in labyrinths.
Was it this date, that? A 1940 census in PA
revealing your middle name as "Damian"
leading to the bare-bone facts. I lucked out.
Even the one typed document--*a résumé*--
buried amongst my papers at the Bienecke. But where?
My memory's useless this point in Time.
I put you in a class
with all the other connoisseurs who've disappeared.
Anyone I knew who knew you
is no longer living. Leads simply drying up.
Yes, you graduated from Yale. Wch class?
Yes, you worked for John Houseman, his wife, Joan for a while.
Yes, I took over from you
mornings helping Virgil Thomson out,
enlightening, fer sure.
But by that time you went on to greater heights
while I made Virgil's portrait on a shoestring camera
not even mine, my very best.
You turned over soil until so many gardens bloom'd in ancien France.
Yes, so many yesses
equal all the dead-ends that lead me back
to where I started on this pen & paper trek
to say I knew you, friend, when you were young once in New York,
not known for being photographed,
                for giving up the ghost.

Bruce Baillie, visionary filmmaker, 1931-2020

Howzit Bruce,
                    What I'm able to retrieve from those 4 decades past 44
is the first remark
you laid on me,
having named your cat after me.
A black & white shorthair domestic,
though I could be off.
The many memories now in flux, compressed.
The many times you stood to fix the angle
of your lens,
as if it were a koan,
as if the light
had to be just right,
to hold the tripod steady,
angling it just so.
Those frames per second, all 24.
The eye never catching up.
No need my telling you.
It was mostly 1 take only moving on,
or so it seems & felt as much
to how the mind's eye frames it,
tracking
weaving
on your eyes' periphery.
I found you where I left you in that dream of movie-stills
is all that now remains
outside your camper
on a hillock in the upper Hudson Valley
one fine brisk day chopping wood.
The leaves on the verge of turning.
The sunlight forever constant.
The sky forever blue.

Edie Sedgwick, superstar, 1943-1971

Edie darling,
        It's been a while, I know. Half a century now, at least.
I made a twilight visit to the Sedgwick Pie
in Stockbridge,
but couldn't pinpoint the tombstone that was yours
in those convoluted circles, those mini-hedges.
The women shunted to the edges.
And yet your memory lingers,
lingering amongst the forlorn,
amongst the many many fans
with dreams born,
born just not yet,
already outliving us.
I believed you when you said,
autumn was your favorite time of year.
You could've told me anywhere
while looking out the window with the twilight coming on.
The Annex eclipsing our silences
while checking out the time:
where to go to get a bite to eat?
Your favorite, L'Avventura,
60th & 2nd Ave.
They still maintain your tab. Your money's good.
Don't even wanna venture guessing what's there now.
New York has ways deleting its own history
until too late to wind back the clock,
even when the page is blank,
even when your words are few.
"My treat," you said.
Your voice still
with that husky drawl
impossible to mimic.
All yours.
All for everything & nothing
when it comes right down to it.
Life's tossed to the winds. We take our chances & we gamble some.
The lives we've lived... and living still.
Where are you now?
Right down the street at Serendipity?
De Noyer, this mysterious boutique mystique?
Where O where is that magic carpet flying to the sky?
The you & you & you,
                the all of you.

Michael McClure, poet & essayist, 1932-2020

Dear Michael,
        You're deserving of a poem. Well, what kind?
Come rain
come shine.
You speak in tongues, that's all,
even howling to a lioness
in the London Zoo.
It's the love that takes you deep. That's why.
To the eagle & the wolf, to the coyute,
the domestic dog, any.
To the fields & streams, the dandelions
where you mingle
with those solitudes
seated underneath a linden tree,
a mighty oak spreading its sweet canopy.
You've kept these outings secret. So be it.
No one really knows
or need to know
who didn't know.
You've played it cool.
You're in your head, your heart too.
You're into wanderings.
The lines come easy as a silent spring
& the everchanging seasons
& the lines too, everchanging.
The snow drips & the wind hawks & owls gamboling.

III
Stories

George Thompson, jazz poet, 1930-

Could it be him? A distant him? A distant second?
A distant likeness, even. That seems about right. Maybe.
He hadda be around 15, maybe 20 years my elder
which would put him in his nineties now.
As handsome as a George Montgomery-type, that 50s yokel
cow-poke type, he was no linesman, no football tackle,
no Hail Mary apropos of his sincerity, his inner yearnings,
all jazzed up as words recited
in the deepest darks of some forgetfulness,
some smoke-filled coffee house, even he'd forgotten.
Even the Mount Eden of those steep back porches,
those far-flung toothpick houses built on stilts.
All those cliff-hanging hikes uphill,
you'd have to stop a moment just to catch your breath.
For this was Cincinnati of the 7 hills,
the city of his birth,
or had I been mistaken? Was it Covington
across the chaste Ohio at its narrowest and shallowest?
Was it anywhere, no less,
than those early morning risers crashed upon
a two-bit breakfast
ham & eggs and coffee piping hot?
Yet he's still nowhere to be found
among those bibliographies, those morning gossamers,
those dead cigarettes singing.
It'll come to me.

Rainer Maria Rilke

Dear Rainer,
        Don't be shy. OK. There's your shy smile
for the camera,
attributed to Stefan Zweig undated,
somewhere taken on the outskirts of Vienna,
I would imagine.
A full new suit. A real necktie
when they were just coming into fashion.
Patent leather loafers peeking through your trousers.
Your arms gently pulling back behind you
in a kind of falcon stoop
and you're very much your lonesome
on a pebbled path in someone's woods.
I could make up all the rest,
but not come close to how you could imagine.
This foto like all the rest might've been destroyed
by Hitler's Youth when they raided Dr. Zweig's library
somewheres between '33 & '34, most likely.
So there's no story to tell.
There's nothing that would keep me wondering.
The twinkle in your eyes tells me that you knew what you were doing
right along between those calming moments, darkling skies,
those everlasting memories by nearly a century of words,
phrases all those dreams separating us,
those dreams that keep us dreaming.

Robert Hayden, Class of 1961?
Univ. of Cincinnati

     I often wonder whatever happened to Robert Hayden,
but that's not true.
My memory's faulty, like stepping off a curb into the blue.
I haven't thought of him in years & years.
What we share might never be remembered.
He was a class ahead of me at Cincinnati. Maybe more.
Was he in pre-med, or was he?
We became fast friends, but I can't remember
why or where, or what was it that we shared?
He was wise in his ways or seemed to be.
He seemed so sure.
He passed all his grades.
He drove an MG roadster with the top down. Vintage.
His pride & joy.
We drove around some nites looking for adventure up at Mt. Eden.
One nite we drove out to his parents' house
on the city's limits.
I don't remember where. Was it a ranch?
We shared a lot in common or it was the camaraderie,
or at least it felt that way,
but now all is lost.
I once encountered him in '75, but seemingly no later.
It was on a stoop in the West Village.
I remember snapping his picture & he was smiling,
but now I have to go find it, if I ever will.
We chatted for a while, and then his presence was no more.
I wonder if he's still around?
Did he make it to safer ground?
I wonder and then I let it go, and still I wonder.

Dorothy Dean, writer, 1932-1987

Dear Dorothy,
           I can't say we were ever friends,
though cross-references abound.
I get lost trying to recount it all, the deadend threads,
and then the anecdotes
get twisted, caught in a brambles in some faded backwater,
or lost in yesterday's news,
the yesteryears piling up.
I seem to recall... it's always
this shortness of memory.
Even the names slip by like some unwoken dream.
Not the dream left behind lurking,
but the names mostly remaining
out of context, boggling any research in the late hours.
I seem to recall you mentioned befriending
Diane di Prima when at Swarthmore.
Why were you telling me this?
I seem to recall you met a former college classmate of mine
through me. I have a picture who he was
his face mostly, in montage,
but still his name escapes me... and that rare, romantic year, no less.
                                          The late '60s?
That seems right.
But what to do with all these disconnects? Is he still living?
Will he leap out the shadows on some lonesome street midi
reminding me, haunting me?
I remind myself of those held dear.
Names you knew them, too, & even better.
Ed Hood, the magnet of Cambridge. *Il Dottore.*
Rosie Blake, sweet Rosie, Radcliffe Class of '63 or was it '62?
Your alma mater.
The archetypal "coffee-date" in Harvard Square
for Doug Kirkland's spread in *Esquire* or was it *GQ* ?
The days of Kodachrome
and those Kodachromed tonalities stay vivid in the mind, those backlit flares,
and Rosie's glowing smile across from me folded hands in hands.
She was & is everlasting. Almost a love story. Almost.
The anecdotes to be completed but never will,
nor what's left to say as much,
remember much. I remember little.
Dorothy? Where art thou now?
The mind plays tricks on the mind.
                        I'm in another world, another life.

Oleg Cassini

Oleg,
      I lost 2--or was it 3--Oleg Cassini sportjackets to the moths & larvae,
the *tineola*, fuck you!
but not the reverence I had when each morning
I'd be greeting you
a neighborly Hello
outside your faux English Gothic castle, East 19th Street,
as you watched over your little dog
whose name escapes me.
Only the late '80s would we remember,
but no later. You'd gone missing
or that we'd ever cross paths again, the famed no-named sidewalk.
The once-familiar presence now more obscure with time.
This stretch of city block becoming lonelier.
Your myth outlived you. Your menswear certainly outlived you
in my closets even when I moved,
or for the stories you could tell me, if you ever could.
The trendy histories,
any number of clouds swiftly passing on a sunlit day.
I never bothered looking up. The *you* I'd recognize,
more distant now with the decades disappearing, all those names, too.
Those brief, those passing moments passing. Now the Olde New York.
                                          Do I got it right?

Wolf Suschitzky, photographer/cinematographer, London, 2016

      The rain was falling steadily, making the streets glisten;
this only happens in springtime London.
I remember Wolfie aka Wolf Suschitzky telling me about this.
Whenever going out
he'd feel his "patience," as he likes to put it
when taking photographs,
especially those candid dark ones:
The girdered gas tank, a favorite location in the East End,
                              looking past the play street,
but there are far & fewer, now between.
The street cleaner somewhat silhouetted in Westminster.
The shoeshine guy on his knees in the Charing Cross Road.
All have this greyless hue
in the sky lingering.
What else there is to do? Take in a movie?
Might as well,
killing time. Isn't that an oxymoron?
This is where I came in after all these years, these decades even.
So I'm lurching into daylight's brightness
blinding me but for an instant.
But no Wolfie! Where is he?! Where's his cane? What, no cane?!
A taxi splashing streams of water nearly misses me!
Got to tell Wolfie about this one,
if he can get it.
That's the BIG secret. Mum's the word till the next poem, maybe.
My imagination still intact can still imagine,
saying to myself aloud,
everything changes; everything remains the same.

Stéphane Mallarmé, fashioniste

      I write across a fashion page, not yet a tearsheet,
not yet yellowed, creased or smudged.
My favorites are the Louis Vuitton ads
with their white spaces filled with white spaces,
reminiscent of Stéphane Mallarmé's last poem, *Un coup de dés...*
He knew what he was doing right along.
He started what was considered the first fashion sheet
with mostly news two columns deep,
by-lined by his Other self,
his ghostly self.
Pen & ink drawings, no photographs.
The rotogravure had yet to be invented.
The *fin-de-siècle* was barely happening.
The tabloid's name slips my mind,
but his mind-set is what's fascinating.
Clothes & poetry.
At 18 my very first poems were captured *objet trouvé* from *Bazaar*.
I saw the poetry glowing in the words
and knew instantly their ambiance.
Those wind-swept dunes.
Those empty highways.
Reflections on the rain-soaked tiles.

In London, 2019

     The news is Clive James, the poet, died after "a long illness"
as reported in *The Guardian* this morning
and another star burns out in the starry heavens.
I've become an habitué in London with my café au lait & frosted bun,
                               my Mont Blanc pen,
in a nearby café filled with stuffed penguins
a doorstep from the Gunnersbury tube stop
where I sit contemplating another unfinished Nicola poem, Nicki for short.
After 3 days of drizzled rain the rain is holding back,
but the skies are still a canvased gray.
The morning long since gone
from the 19th century.
The skies no less the same over the mighty Hudson.
My library remains forever peaceful in their morning louvered light.
My 3 cats in repose with their hungry eyes, their Cheshire smiles
the way I picture them this very moment
a long ways from home.
And where is home away from poems
waiting to be discovered.
Jimmy Page, I haven't seen him in years & years.
His smiling face endearing still. God bless him still.
I remain forever faithful to the Word.
No way to turn back the past
or fast-forward the near future where old news is re-awakened.

James Fox, British movie star

James Fox once said Hello to me across the lobby of the Algonquin
as he was passing through, *circa?*
With his nitty-gritty smile. No kidding.
I've not the faintest where he was dashing to.
It could've been some starry dream in the middle of a carnal New York afternoon,
or a subway ride rattling towards some sort of Bronx daylight rushhour,
or he'd be studying the script,
getting into character for *Performance,*
or for the sequences to be photographed, rephotographed
fulfilling Roeg's vision
of those darkest hours darker still
until there's no way knowing what's in store
between the high road & the low in dreamy Chiswick.
Did he swing
his way through high heaven,
breaking into song when least expected? I've yet to wonder.
The truest light is when the kleigs switch off,
and the palest hues
sublimate those noonday glows,
those silent roads
lurching towards a nowhere heaven,
and suddenly a downpour
comes pouring through.
What's in a name when you mistake a name for nowhere else to go?
You kidding me?
How do I address thee?
How do I undress thee?
It so happens such sounds such as they are,
lead to a darkened wood
of echoes, flashes, not much of anything, leaves fallen.
When does a tap dance routine reflect a dénouement
of happenstance? I'm getting sleepy.
There's lots more to do.
One of those noonday dog day afternoons
when not much happens, happens.
I've not a clue.
I've not a quid to spare.
The stories that surround you surround me too.

patti smith, poet

Darling patti good morning patti,
                         I don't even know wch way to turn.
My 1st inkling is to race off to the Café Flore
to meet you in the falling rain
among the ghosts still lingering.
No need to name-drop,
you know them all.
We know them by their names, their cursive scripts.
I've made the Flore my home away from home, and you have too, I know.
I feel safest & secure
and right next door even a lonesome bookshop
lures me in, where in 2015 was it I got *Just Kids* in French, Denoël
just for the heck of it.
How French is that?!
The Flore couldn't be more French
when past the blue awning it rains a gusting rain, a Paris rain.
You run for cover.
You dash right in
looking for the nearest table.
Croissants & café crème.
You hug the mug just to keep your hands warming.
The Herald-Tribune spread out on your table. It's now the Times.
Times have changed.
Paris makes my day when I'm in Paris. All of it.
Your email makes my morning, too.
                         Next time... next time.

Dreaming from 4 to 6 in the morning.

Not Another Sonnet?!

    The snows of yesteryear and yesterday car-high and shoulder-high.
Remember when? No, I don't remember when!
I don't wanna care which way the past is blowing in,
which way it goes to its never-ending end,
                                  its deep crevasse.
The memories of friends are friends fewer still,
are yet another memory loss.
But what's this gotta do with those claustrophobic winters?
Everything is white, pure white--we know it's white!--
until it turns a bluer blue as dusk sets in,
until the sky turns a topsy-turvy kaleidoscopic hue.
The best dreams occur from 4 to 6 some mornings I've often said.
They never fail. That still holds true.
When will I find my way beside the crackling fire, my tomes of books?
Where is the shining path beneath all that snow?
Did I after all write down the wrong address out of memory loss?
Not another no-no!
Memories emerging out of primal darkness
return again herein,
and here again herein remains a deeper loss.
                            Don't tell anyone.

for Jean Wainwright

The Sunday Funnies

I won't read about you in the Sunday papers.
I won't read the obscure facts,
the telling truths,
those darknesses at noon,
or as a comic-strip, *Tim Tyler's Luck* perhaps
before his luck runs out but never did.
Never never never until my voice grows hoarse.
"We have no real language for death," as Henry Miller so remarked.
Only the to-and-fro, the golden hours,
those storytelling ghosts.
Sometimes life is an illusion
whereas the movies it's not.
                  How's that, I wonder?
I remember a phrase which haunted me when I was younger:
"Follow your nature to be happy," and so I did,
which also led me closer to your memory than to you.
In nature it was all the more so.
Sometimes in looking up I'd stare through
silhouetted sleepers at the open sky beyond.
My dreams were only bygone summer whispers,
                               summer breezes.

Touching the Marvelous

I'm saving the kitty-litter for last, ha-ha,
the last thing I wanna do before day's end.
Sometimes the memories of those now gone is burdensome.
Sometimes it's miles and miles of sleep before I wake,
or of a desert in my dreams
that doesn't seem to wanna go away.
And now the focus is
massaging Zazie's right front paw
to stave off an arthritic tenderness advancing.
I give it my faith.
The poetry can wait, but who am I kidding?
That's what I'm doing right now!
And I'm not even halfway to the end.
Am I making any sense?
What is the end?
There's no end to poetry, I've been told.
Did M. Valéry tell me this?
Am I making any headway with the hands-on I'd been taught so long ago?
The knowledge to do well. The knowledge
where & when
it's needed when entering a calm state unexplained,
a quietude under some shaded linden tree
to touch the marvelous,
to make of it a magic carpet in my dreams,
to hold back time's waking,
even if it means no différence
between the dream and the waking.

To sleep, perchance to dream...

In the dream your voice grows increasingly distant.
And as this poem awakens from the dream,
it's now a real poem all its own.
If I don't write it down, I'll forget
and I'd be lost. I need points of reference,
the names of the Tube stops,
parks we've crossed together in the London twilight,
your favorite café,
your favorite restaurant or two.
The great crowdings along Oxford Street noontime.
The last movie we saw at the BFI.
The one-week road-trip to the feisty cliffs of Cornwall.
The many snapshots along the way.
The country churchyards. The rustic inns. The quietudes.
As in any one instant the dream I'm having
ends suddenly without any tangible trace to your existence
and I wake up empty. Who's there?
A poem no one will ever get the chance to read. Ghostly. Luminescent.
Or: who were they? someone asks in passing.
I couldn't understand why I can't remember,
as if such memories had been hibernating and then thumped awake;
a set of circumstances catching up with you in the purple haze.
"We should return here more often," I could barely hear you say above the din
of the onrushing street traffic.
But knowing this now sets up its own déjà vu.
Moments overlapping moments when I feel anxious,
unable to write them down instantly
and fearful I'd forget
when ten years hence I could barely read my own handwriting
much less certain words accidentally smudged out, illegible. It's a mess.
Before and *after* are but a dream in dream time
                              that continues and then simply stops.

Richard Poirier, literary critic & editor, 1925-2009

Dear Richard, Professor Poirier,
                          Whenever I try I fail imagining
where we must've been,
preventing us from crossing paths,
or on some windswept dusty street.
These historic leaps,
landing us in some Godforsaken dive
of the kind Wystan Auden
found himself in 1939
in the tightly-knit West Fifties.
More like some long lost weekend of the high humidities.
Suddenly I've passed the threshold where dreams leave off at 6:00 a.m.,
and now it's 6:08, 8 minutes past.
Zazie in the next room speaks to me in her chirping sounds.
And I'm still waking, asking: Where am I? Am I
short of breath?
                          Can't fully grasp the vacant imagery.
The street sounds whooshing past,
searching my pockets for a matchbook lost address.
My own darkness keeps folding in in stages.
I'll not know when it comes.
I'll be rid of all those backaches, finally.
All those leg aches,
those radiating aches. The ennui.
Those great expectations or acceptance speeches. Ha-ha.
Who's kidding whom?
The teeth problems.
The lyme-induced suspicions.
My own obit, if there is one. Wishful thinking,
or the last time I saw Paris.
The last time I glanced down at my little Cartier
for all those missed appointments sorely missed.
The last time I opened the kitchen cabinet
forgetting why I did this.
Forgetting & remembering.
What's past? What's next? What's sleep? What's life about?
I seem to lose the thread. I've not the answer *why*.
Forgetting to switch the light on... no need to.
The dawn is dawning... seems I'm stuck in this dizzy *déjà vu*.

6:22 a.m.

I've gone beyond the expectant time of dreaming and now no dreams.
There are no first names, even.
No greetings on the street. No emails. What I've done the day before.
My memories like a sieve
through which nothing I can get a grasp on
happens. The words well-placed, those that have survived.
And then what to do with them?
Stretching out those sentences for as far as they would go,
across those yellow sheets of paper, the lines well-placed.
Or else nothing happens.
I'm suddenly in a lurch
to rise up outta bed
or drift back to sleep for another search
without seeing in the dark. Without knowing what to ask.

Early Morning Dream

What are those times within me to remember--to not forget?
What are those 2-hours worth dreaming
and of the dreamless state after and before?
The many poems attest to it.
Should I be amazed?! Should I be absent-minded?
The many many years, the many decades
at a faster pace than last imagined,
like an unnamed clipboard list,
like footnotes gone awry, confused, and hyper.
Those mornings spent in reverie.
The sacrosanct of times as words emerging syllabically in sentences.
Lines falling off the page like some cartoon road-runner with dust billowing.
The stream of consciousness becoming anarchies of words.
The histories somersaulting through a darkened cabaret, footloose & fancy-free.
The rhythms sounding like the click-e-ty of grinding trains not known where.
It takes arriving, it takes care
to stay the schedule,
to be true-blue to what the dream apprehends, persisting.
All dreams ensnared resisting
memory in those slumberings within.

Robert Duncan, poet, 1919-1988

Robert, that you?
          I woke up this morning and thought I was dead
or on my way to some darkened plain
where the closest mountain
wasn't reachable, even deep in dreamland.
That's how achy my body was--and still is,
feeling the after-effects of sleeping on my right side--
perhaps my wrong side, after all,
as the arthritis clings to every joint.
But that's not all.
My synapses are severing,
but in a so-so lackadaisical pace.
Soon as remembering something important comes into play,
another remembrance diminishes before the noonday
glare starts its downward spiral.
So many instances forgotten or misplaced,
like the 14 Bernard Heidsieck letters
or the Jim Carroll negatives, for all their worth.
Can't lose sleep over this.
At least my dreams emerge uncluttered by time
and the so-called mortal time remaining.

Poem to Myself

What if suddenly I wasn't here anymore?
What if I died in my sleep,
or died of "failing health," like they say,
in all those obits.
Even Zazie Sasha Xena in their purring sleep beside me
won't know I'm gone... or will they?
Here one morning, gone the next.
The poems remain, even the 2nd rate ones, like this one.
You wake up one morning with the knowledge of your non-existence,
helpless on the outside looking in,
helpless to change things for the better.
You can't switch on the bedside lamp.
You can't finish the book you've been reading.
You can't even turn on the computer.
Ah, a first instance of modern times.
In dreams there are no responsibilities made mentioning
as I'm nearing that 4 a.m. threshold,
that ha-ha moment where dreams tend to coalesce, sometimes.
I never told you so.
There simply wasn't time. I blacked out or I whited out.
There's no bail in life.
No more helloes, goodbyes.
You become a stranger to your fate.
You become what you once were, if remembered, even.

Autumnal breezes

I'm lucky if I can connect with my subconsciousness,
even on a weekly basis anymore,
or suspend my disbelief stringing words together
from what's previously accepted as the norm,
whether twilight was a fever for those scattered dreams
or as a place letting loose what silences remain,
what gossamers sway entangled
entangled in those trees. What dreams abound,
what instances shift their fade-ins/fade-outs as if
as if no proof of their existence still remaining,
as if *I told you so,*
but didn't tell you so. Didn't
for a moment turn back at those darkened woods
for that glimmered light, that sudden lurching of autumnal breezes.

Oubli

What am I to do with this *oubli,* this blank

which has entered my life

as reminder that I'm a poet some of the time,

not all of the time.

What happens at those other intersections,

that a certain remembered image coincides with the continuity of moments, a
                                        certain truth,
when suddenly I'm turning a street corner

on the rue Burgundy

and find myself lost in an entirely unfamiliar neighborhood

than the one I was in just yesterday

and the struggle to find my way back to safer ground.

But when I reach there the street's flooded

with a colonnade of palms & crazy hedges,

and it was only a dream, after all. Can this be right?

And it wasn't yesterday or just yesterday.

It was yesterday late afternoon precisely

I'd woken from a long slumbered nap

and the hazy outdoor light awaited me.

The oft-chance

It's 6:03.
I gotta take a pee.
I gotta fight my way back to where those dreams await me Fellini-like.
Where did I leave off?
What was the last thread?
Ach!!! It'll all come back to me some other way,
some new dimension cinematically.
It's already 6:12!
This ain't gonna work.
Time has already passed what I wanna say.
Time works fast.
Damn, I'm wide awake!
when I'd rather be wide asleep.
Those expanses awaiting me, those desert wastes.
Not much to say.
No other way.
That's not true.
I can trick myself to sleep.
I've done that before.
I wanna sneeze. I catch my breath.
I catch my breath. I don't.
What's going on here?!
                              Where did I leave off...

Not Another Sonnet!

Soon, I will run outta words at any given wintry morning,

especially in those last remaining minutes

when the light forces through the blinds, scaring off Sasha, Zazie, even baby Xena.

Or standing on a shunned & dingy platform

waiting for the next local upon those shiny rails

with the station lights still dimming flickering.

And the same rusty stains smeared across the tiles,

still remaining where they were years past.

I will still fumble in the dark for pen & paper while holding on to sleep.

I will still hold back memory

for fear of losing all those sentences caught in a net of dreamy synapses.

Sooner or later, I will have to take a pill collapsing short-term into long-term memory,

remembering those words making way for more words,

more sentences, more silences, and love, the singular.

I must stay healthy. I must be aware at all times when something drops,

when something falls outta my breast pocket,

or when I'm stepping down a flight of stairs.

I must be optimistic, I am and then some.

One poem at a time,

one photo, then some.

What does ...*and then some* hold dear?

What are the secrets? *Love?* Words camouflaged?

Not to give away too much:

The golden curtain parted in a city called Oz.

And where is Oz, or for a happiness held dear?

That lonesome train yard of my childhood...

where do all these trains go on their morning runs?

Shunted one track to another,

open to the rattling rains, the sleepy sleets, the snows?

I rub my eyes. I'm sitting in those midnites by a kitchen lamp sometimes flickering,

as words emerge flickering, remembering... and I wander and I wander far.

A night glows long past my sleep when a dream takes over,

timeless in a sleep that never stirs.

Dream, 17:VI:19

There was very little I could recount from the night before.
In fact, it was more like 5:34.
When I turned to read the clock,
the light was not streaming in my window.
It was a greyish overcast with bits of sunlight slipping through.
So I didn't have to take down the Karen Radkai & the Duchamp. No UV glare.
I tried to pinpoint the mouse on an airport somewhere
in Brooklyn for a flight taking me to Paris.
Jean was by my side as we made our way to the departure gate.
There was much I was leaving behind and the flat in Paris was not all that expensive.
This, it was assumed, would be my home
with fabrics on the wall.
What would I do when I arrived?
I hadn't a clue.
I hadn't a clue about anything.
Life, it appeared, was nearing its last phase.
The songbirds outside my window were whistling their songs to get me up.
Time to feed the cats.
Time to forget all I struggled to recount.
Time to start all over.

Félix

Félix,
> I don't get to pat you on the head or even kiss you, snuggle you,
you beast! or even talk to you.
Obviously, our conversations remain one-sided.
And then, what would I say: Nothing about you was ever simple,
especially for a 10-year-old?
The histories following you & surrounding you
are many, the many times & chases, unrecollected mostly,
just as childhood fades
& fades
& fades.
> I'll just take your word for it, if only
you'd speak to me, even a mee-ow would do.
But what would I do with those tonalities?
What could you tell me
to encourage me, embrace those moments of discovery & disarray
that could reincarnate you
into the cat I knew
from those childhood days marvelling your antics
in those darkened matinees
5-minutes at the most, as we speak in tongues,
as we dream each other's dreams in montage
with you not there, with you
as memory for another dreamy darkness.
The language we once shared, and share again,
> one deep stare or two.

Awe

There was no oral tradition when I was growing up.

There was no way retrieving memory from those deep dreams,

nor any future that would point the way, this or that.

One day at a time led to the next and to the next.

I invented games.

I collected what caught my eye. All sorts of cards.

I watched obscure movies on TV. I had my favorites.

I read Donald Duck and the monthly movie magazines.

I immersed myself in cinematic dreams.

Everywhere I turned, I was infinitely curious.

Every newsstand corner held a secret.

Every subway ride took me far & wide.

The awe of life awaited in those daylight days,

never likely to have known those stirrings.

Dream dreaming

It appears like the cold front would last forever.
Would you stop it already?!
No, it's true!
I tried to cover myself with the one bedsheet
and the cats stared at me
like I was crazy
and curled up with each other to gather warmth.
It felt like somebody was chasing me through the night.
He looked like a dishevelled academic
with his shirttails trailing,
maybe wanting his picture taken.
I reached an impasse in the pursuit.
A staircase crumbled
and I managed climbing over the debris.
It slowed things down a bit.
I arrived at this very noisy party.
There were 2 people gone missing in the crowd I couldn't ID.
Everyone kept going round & round like they were on a carousel and joyful.
I was stationed on a wooden folding chair.
No one paid me any heed.
I was in the middle of a darkened city. Was it London?
My legs were hurting me.
It was 6:21 when I reached daylight.

l'eclisse

      Where is the faith I hope I've had
going? Those rainy day musings
when as a kid I'd stare out the window
at a glimpse of nothing in particular, except a rain-reflected street of lights & darks,
trees swaying in a gentle breeze.
An empty space more dark than light
where once a thoroughfare
existed, existing still,
but with no specific sense
of where such roads lead on,
diverging from each other.
Will they be the same, look the same
as I grow older? When
is that, I wonder.
Time pushes me to the edges, especially when I'm napping.
Where is this poem taking me? Why now?
Those tinted cityscapes, once familiar, now more picturesque
as cartes de vistite in an album.
Friends' names have vanished to the point of no return
where nuances were more familiar,
where the living was easy,
now not so much.
I'm suddenly feeling lighter in the head.
Is this an early sign something's not going right?
Will I wake another day to find it's not another day,
but the same as yesterday
                        or the day before?

The lesson of life is for me to follow my nature to be happy.
Then leave me alone
to do my thing,
words in other words a flashflood of emotion,
in a downpour Paris,
in those gentle Irish rains.
I am the embodiment of "mutable water,"
      so I'm told by Tad, my astrologer & friend.
I am myself & not myself.
I wake into the day with the past left far back behind me in the wings.
The Central Park Mall a Charles Ives reminiscence.
The Bowery station a memory where no one gets on or gets off.
The departing train remains within an après echo.
The 3rd Avenue El a memory that my childhood had embraced.
All those shadows slipping through the sleepers way above.
All those trolleys left out in the icy glaze.
Those movies long since gone in a darkness also lost.
The words lost, the words found, also lost.
Happiness is the seed to more happiness.
Sometimes a light points the way,
sometimes a shadow,
               also the dark side of the light.

Zazie 3

Every morning when I crawl back into bed as the clock nears 6,
thus shutting down any remnants from the night,
the 4 to 6 a.m. slot
when dreams are at their best & do their tricks,
Zazie grooms herself to Queneau's delight. Mine, too.
First, her back legs outstretched like a sleepy ballerina
to better reach them with her tongue;
then her shoulders. Then I forget which.
Is this her way telling me we're getting ready
for a nite out on the town?
Zazie! what can I tell you of the night before,
or of a life, as if my life simply opens with an *a*?
But there's only so much I can convey.
Wch one will hold your eyes wide-eyed all the more
till you get bored
with all this baby talk,
deciding to skidoo,
and now I'm left alone with my one life.
Who else can I talk to
at this shut-eye hour when not even the bluebirds are singing me their song?
Sometimes I wonder if my life is one vast desert emptiness
where ships have met their end littering the coastline facing west.
Sometimes I wonder, then I don't.
There are dreams
still undreamt until I beckon them.
Will they come true?
Will they remain true...
and then I forget.
I've forgotten much, Zazie, what little's left.
I cherish all the rest.
I cannot count the ways,
cannot count the days & what those nites will bring,
what to recall
or is it all
                one click away? The many secret poems.
                                    The scratchy photographs.

Sunday Sunday

Dear heart, that's me!
          It's now 6 a.m. Nothing enlightening occurred the nite before.
No words turning into lines illuminated,
and no remembrance,
loss,
relationships,
the sudden melancholy that grips the soul
and won't let go,
and now Sasha's me-owing his way up the stairs dragging his feathered toy.
What a boy!
It's chilly outside. All bundled up in bed
as if I'm an Inuit.
What news awaits me in the Sunday Times?
What Acts of God will I discover, then write across the page?
Will there be anyone I know or knew or anyone obscured?
It's now 6:04. Another hour to go, maybe
if I can catch some shut-eye, maybe
I can catch some remnants what's left remaining.
No achy legs. That's a good sign.
Princess Zazie curled up asleep in her feline dreams. I can see her twitching.
Will we meet in each other's dreams?
I'm sure it's happened, but I can't recall.
I let her be, my sweetheart.
The stream of the unconscious hasn't reached its consciousness plateau.
I'm hurtling forward into day.
I'm optimistic. Happy.
Yet it's still dark outside. Its après moon
like a sprayed background.
Daylight Saving Time I guess is on the wane.
Poetry for me is so unpredictable & incurable,
more like an addiction
especially when I slip into its trance,
I need the therapy. I'm astonished!
And now Sasha climbs into bed with his handsome face.
God bless him. There's nothing hurtful in his soul,
the soulful centered in his hazel eyes.
The morning slowly unfolds
          and I am blessed.

Bob Dylan's cat?

　　　It could've been Paul Eluard's cat.　Did he have a cat?
Was it Walter Chandoha's cat?
Was it Bob Dylan's cat?
That was the end of that.
I can't remember another poem of Bob's where he cites a cat.
The dream is far darker than my imagination allows me
to perceive with any certainty.
But between 5 & 6 within the predawn light,
the remnant of a line--was it the last line?--remains blurry for one instant...
and then slips into a slow slow dissolve.
So my sleep state can't catch these few words flickering
above the note-pad by my bed
until the only word remaining is the word *cat*.
It's as if the word itself is a kind of vernacular,
as if Bob said *skidoo* to the cat
perched in an armchair,
like he wanted to sit by the fire to keep warm,
and then the dream cat cuts out,
and I have no way knowing if the cat
had actually leapt off the chair,
or was the cat actually real, after all.
Was it a way of posing
or reposing, as felines classically do.
Bob had ended his poem with the word *cat,*
And the words preceding were like a string of jewels or stars.
He was there in the room all right and yet he seemed absent
and the poem remains untitled.
It was up to me to give it one.
I leave the poem as is.
　　　　　　　　The poem is left guessing.

Marisa Berenson as she appears in The Guardian, 30:X:19

Marisa darling,
             I'm not sure you ever appeared in a dream of mine
the way you've appeared in real life.
The unconscious stretching into morning's consciousness
suspending those disbeliefs, *réalité.*
Was it one take? Two? I hope not. The fade-ins, fade-outs.
More like a dozen, maybe three!
You keep getting better
with each astonishment, each stride, sure-footed. I could tell.
Each episode shared,
if I could remember it all. Every nuance,
every minute rained on as we rush for cover 'cross the cobblestones.
The blvd Saint-Germain in a spree.
Was it the blue awning at the Café Flore?
Was it the local grocery in your neighborhood or was it mine?
The locales mesh into one
until they reappear in a Utrillo, had he painted one.
Come back, little sheba,
remembering things past the hour of midnite.
Those reflections that brighten our lazy days, further on.
The names of friends still echoing, whispering.
Those dusky dusks with the backlit flares that last
past the turning of leaves,
but for a few brief moments vivid, eternal, beyond us.

Some days I feel the death of me...

Some days I feel the death of me, like it could all come crashing down
upon my head.
I'm living alone, me & my 3 cats.
What would become of them?
My library,
my artworks on the walls, some still wrapped in bubble-wrap.
The clamshells filled with fotos neatly labelled.
The research files.
The postcards, the movie-stills.
Very little paper correspondence. Yale got it all.
Lots of email printouts. Who knew?
All those projects planned ahead.
What else, who else?
The many many friends, far & wide.
You come into the world with a brain & with a heart
and that's the most one can hope for with the years until it's time.
But one never knows the time.
Will it rain today?
I check the weather.
What's there to say or left to say?
I feel sluggish.
My bones ache.
Will they talk to one another
the way all sorts of tree roots communicate
through a kind of earthly telepathy?
The roots of heaven now of the earth.
I always wanted to build a model train layout as a kid.
Sadly, never got around to doing it.
My most extravagant dream was to sail on a real oceanliner
across the Atlantic in a Bob Peak ad along the Lido Deck.
Just remember at a moment when I come to mind
or in your sleep.

Poem for my dad, Gerardo aka Jerry, 1897-1983

When I woke I couldn't imagine where my dad had been sleeping
in the house.
It took some contemplating where he was.
His presence was that prescient.
The upstairs hallway lights had been left on.
I could've sworn I turned them off.
I don't remember why Sasha was meowing so much, on & on.
Did something spook him?
He climbed on top of me, as if
I were his mountain & he the chartreux lion.
In his eyes I was.
His eyes looked hungry. Had he been fed?
I was under the covers when I woke
& now I'm wide awake.
The words come uneasily.
The gray outside my bedroom window was still a grayish gray.
It hadn't rained yet,
nor will it still.
There was this eerie feeling I was very much alone,
& yet Jerry's presence
wouldn't go away, as if
he'd be appearing any moment now,
looking in to see if I'm okay or simply drowsy.
I couldn't figure
what the next book would be that I was reading.
It just wasn't happening
the way I'd been expecting answers,
words defying definition,
meanings flashed across a movie screen
escaping, fading, slowly disappearing.
I'm at a loss simply to know more.
I'm at a loss for dropping things & then dropping things.
That damn cane, for instance!
I'd be leaning it against the wall one moment
and no sooner than I turn my back,
it comes crashing to the floor. *Merde!*
I welcome sleep even when I'm not sleepy-eyed.
I go on & on, as if
nothing mattered at that moment.
The days come back to haunt me, as do
those autumn afternoons sometime, too.
There are dreams waiting to be had,
to be continued. Where is my dad?

Did I leave him far behind, if at all,
lost in a dream of mine, also lost.
I yearn for those silences to come.
I yearn to wake & yet I wanna search for where my dreams come true
or for the one name,
                    the one muse I keep secret. I forget.

Gregg Barrios, playwright

Dear Gregg,
                    I'd made a decision a while back that I'd disembark
                                at the Fordham Road
rather than take the train all the way into Grand Central.
What's an Interurban doing on a local El track anyways...
& then I went on.
I'd exit in The Bronx.
I was familiar with the streets, familiar
with the trolley tracks,
the shoppes all brilliantly displayed with housewares, Venetian glass, tchotchkes.
I hear echoes of passersby calling out my name.
I skip along, alone now
but not alone.
Someone led the way whom I've never seen before.
He was singing a song I'd not heard, clustering with rhymes.
I followed him a while
and then realized I'd left my reading glasses behind,
but didn't stop & turn around.
Was he an animus? Some long lost soul?
What was he to me I'd never know,
as I made a steep jump from a boardwalk edge,
but didn't feel the impact when I landed, gliding down.
But he was far too far ahead for me to catch up,
and then he disappeared.
                            I woke up.
It's Sunday morning nearing 8 o'clock.
Time to get up, feed the kitties.
I'm in a different world than when I started out.
I hear this ringing in my ears.
I remain cautious should a vertigo suddenly appear.

Jean Cocteau, renaissance man, 1889-1963

M. Cocteau,
            I've had several false starts over the years, catching up
with what I didn't know about you till 1959,
or even earlier with your movie in the snow, the French snow.
The Blood of a Poet. How'd you manage that?!
Two days from now, snow's predicted,
sweeping down across the Kaaterskills.
When I was growing up... well, I'm still growing up
with every new line of poésie.
Ever see those MGM musicals?
What?! No mail today?!
No news is good news, as they say.
In your day you'd be getting tons of letters through the slot
with all those pretty cancelled stamps,
all those élégant embellishments.
This morning I found an Abe Lincoln copper penny dated 2020 heads up
in the slime & muck.
Maybe it'll bring me luck.
A throwback when I was Italian superstitious. Still am.
The Lilly Prize. I do my Walter Mitty.
Miss Lilly: *She knew a thing or two about rejection,*
make-believe, walkin' in the rain,
walking in those darkened woods for inspiration.
Those diving owl hoots & whistles,
bringing music to my ears.
When as a kid growing up,
I'd take these sunset walks with my Uncle Joe,
past where Tiemann Ave ended in The Bronx.
It was all woods back then, c. 1948 or 1950.
Now try finding them, in this day & age.
Try as hell to blink your eyes.
I'm still here, not yet the poet that I am without a prize.
I'm at the very stoop,
the very house where Uncle Joe/Aunt Dolly lived.
The very house depicted in my very 1st photograph
rediscovered in a shoebox recently.
The ephemera of dust & my very birth certificate.
The vellum's whittled at the edges.
Still readable.
Still stating all the facts, but no mention of my varied futures
when looking back in retrospect,
I remember you, M. Jean.
Just another name
with those photogenic hands.
The curiosity embracing you that glows within you.

M. Rimbaud

Arthur,
   In my reimaginings, you were nowhere close to the 16-year-old
poet-to-be, the prodigal of Paris
and now no closer in that self-portrait taken in Aden
unrecognizable in 1883, or is it '84?
"I think that I'm aging myself terribly," you said.
And within a year or two
you high-tailed it outta Roche, the Ardennes, for good,
your patrimony,
& walked in fear through desert wastes
& local wars & hither regions far beyond,
working in the trade of trading goods: "Dried leathers,
ivory, feathers, rubber, incense, coffee, bulks of tea."
Everything was ink & inkwells.
Beasts of burden.
A world of ambiances.
The dreadful heat of summer. "Stifling!"
"I have gastric fever. I can't digest a thing, and so it goes."
The letters to Maman prove exceptional.
The words drifting further from the source that made you
dream to be a *seer,* to speak in tongues.
        Well, that never happened.
Where's the solace in all of this? Where's the hope
as you drift in & out of focus?
Arthur, there's no way you could've heard me calling out.
It's 4:15 my time. Still very dark.
Time to dream, if they come in the weee hours.
My cats curled up asleep.
It's winter here in the Kaaterskills.
Yes, you've aged. You're not looking well.
One morning late you woke up
from some lowly nightmare
to the nightmare having lost a leg
       and then you died.

Aram... Aram Saroyan, poet

Dear Aram, hi buddy,
              We haven't spoken in a while.
Sometimes we'd go for months,
& then come full circle round.
A throw of the dice for *poésie.* I owe you one.
The walk around the block, the fire escapes in silhouette.
The film noir of later years that we embrace.
The friendships shared,
fewer now. No less loved.
No less remembered.
No less the dreams,
heading out for lunch on uptown Madison.
Your neighborhood. The Schrafft's sundaes sipping straws.
The focus sometimes getting fuzzy round the edges.
Don't you agree?
As do the names
we've come to know.
The shared intimacies
& now the empty chairs.
We count our blessings
& our poems
& our snapshot histories,
even trading foto secrets.
The course of life.
The simplicity & grace. It just is.
We keep it cool.
All we know & can ever know.
4:18, no, 4:19.
This is the time returning to the dream,
or where & when we give the poem a rest.
Or walking round the pool table lining up the killer shot
anticipating miracles, life follows us.
That, too, takes a certain talent, a certain cool.
Beauty in the gesture.
              We let it be.

Leigh Taylor-Young, movie star

Dearest Leigh, dearest you,
                              What I remember still is not so much
the movies you starred in,
excepting *Soylent Green* ha-ha, for all the wrong reasons
but for the "real" you off-screen.
The never ever make-believable you
beyond the blue
& for the one lone jet-black Jasper who took to you
and when that happens, you don't forget
while he's *in character*
taken to
the rooftop of your spiffy sports coupe
some forlorn driveway
near the Sunset Strip,
far, far from those memories
for lack of better word
we share,
if we ever will, if & when we will. Somewhere
in those exits those entrances, like
may I take your hand,
may I have this dance?
Yet the words escape me, fading out. Please forgive me
my forgetfulness, my superfluous....
Take 1.
Take 2.
        No, that will never do.

Gerry Gelb, teenage friend, c. late 1950s.

Dear Gerry,
      Was it Gerry with a "G" or with a "J"?
My mind's a blank.
You came to me in a dream or rather your absence did.
Been 62 years approximately.
I've a vivid memory what you looked like,
or I think I do.
You were the holy terror.
A perpetual 5 o'clock shadow before it was ever fashionable.
But for some Godforsaken reason unexplained,
the words betray me.
Nothing to cling to. Nothing
I could relate to,
that in my mind you did exist. Wait!
There was a letter you'd written me, 20 years back
from out of nowhere's land.
Typewritten w/ several stupid typos.
A return address that didn't seem to wanna work
somewhere in Ohio.
The letter was returned, insufficient or expired.
The chain was broken.
Did I place it in the Beinecke where it might get lost?
Or is it somewhere in the house?
And you're drifting as before.
The facts were scanty.
I assume we're the same age.
You might've been a bit older or younger by a year at most.
I don't know. I can only guess,
like all the rest.
Existential, or non-existential.
The more I forget I try to cling to,
like in a dream once dreamt
is lost on waking,
like a love,
if one can call it that.
A love of words, more likely;
but even here I hit a snag, a dead-end,
like the street you lived on with your dad.
That much I'm certain. Tiebout Ave... or was it Elm Place?
Obscure at its northern end dead-ending Fordham Road
                    in an unexpected blizzard.
An intersection that bisected nothing. Not us.
We were always somewhere else,
but even these names elude me,
like the ghost you've now become.

Your presence but an absence.
Nowhere to turn.
Nowhere to run.
Is it a street of shoppes all boarded up, where you are now?
A shopping mall, if there's one still? Is it,
was it Cleveland?
Your death as obscure as was your life.
I could delete that, but I won't.
There's no living proof otherwise. Nothing tangible.
Not one snapshot, even... or a même.
Where art thou, then,
I ask the shadow on the wall graffiti-like.
I wake with a ringing in my ears,
                              but that's nothing I wanna hear.

A genuine epiphany

Virginia Woolf, July 1902

You know, Ginia,
                that's what your dad called you,
I could knock you off your feet if I had to.
Do I want to... ha-ha,
on off-days staring through that leaded upstairs window
at those rolling foaming sweeping waves
with only hints of echoings
overlooking St Ives Bay
as I catch you in a state of *rêverie,*
for all those hours past, those decades even, separating us.
Simply no way reaching back in time in reaching you,
re-writing history even.
Well, that's not true.
There are many many dreams between 4 & 6 bewitching you
& me. Had I not told you?
Any one of them you've appeared suddenly.
"Astonish me!"
And you've astonished me
in that nearly full-profile
you've given me as with all of you,
as suddenly you turn away
at that undecisive moment
when the snapshot clicked immortalizing you,
but never meaning to.
"Ginia, where are you, darling?"
Sometimes a picture reveals far more past
that instant of distracted revelation.
I can touch you on the neck, how's that?!
That swan's down neck *parfumed,*
shouldered by that soft white linen smock.
And so I breathe in deep
and hold it all... well, not all,
the way you've held that pose, then let it go.
I'm always photographing you & jostling with you.
I've yet to let you laugh,
but I've not shot that shot yet nor now.
Where is *now?*
You're too quick for me,
and I for you!
Let's hold each other's silences until it's time to dream & sleep
                in which to save it all.

The New Mélancholia

Trailblazing histories

Dear us,
          Who'd ever imagine a history in the making & then some?
The telltale remnants of a photograph, or some photomatiques.
That certain slant of sunlight no longer certain
nor even slanting
right there in my lens I'd seen it,
actively imagined it
with you on some childhood swing.
The one decisive frame still waiting.
I was trying to remember when we first met. London Photo,
dashing from one gallery to the next.
My eye(s) catching you than all the "art" assembled. Or was it
the chatty cafeteria where we sat across each other.
You surrounded by your Oxford friends.
Me immersed in the far-off *coup de foudre.*
What I remember is always of a moment,
the gentle repose and words words a faulty 2nd for what remains
the essence how all things started, the circumstances
we'd been given, given the time allotted.
The stream of consciousness disintegrating. Sentences dissembling.
"A THROW OF THE DICE NEVER NEVER WILL ABOLISH CHANCE,"
so said Mallarmé, facing the morning odds out at the races.
A ha-ha moment settles in.
                      Time still chases us.

Étonnez-moi!

Why do I keep feeling this "dialogue of the mind with itself"*
in your absence...
I could easily equate this with telepathy.
I surprise myself sometimes.
It's not like moving mountains mind you.
Even a bit more like being light-hearted left-handed
until things happen unexpectedly simpatico.
A synchronicity of sorts,
the rendezvous we were planning
I knew wasn't gonna be. How? I had a hunch.
I'm clairvoyant. That's all.
It comes in handy when taking your picture with the light continually bouncing
off 4-storey windows, then 3, then 2
with that heavenly shine.
You astonish me sometimes,
all those dreams, a slow
raft of emails, a whole lot more
and then the flight to London. Where to begin?
Those "emotions recollected in tranquility." Those domesticities.
Those dialogues I'm having with the absentee-you,
then back to 2,
then a quietude ensues
for that one brief instant
and then one Sunday we go walking in the Sunday woods, those spooky woods,
those *petits bonheurs,*
those hands migrating in their warmth
and we lose all sense of time. It's 11:11.
A slumbered dream, fer sure.
The mind drifting off finally.

Matthew Arnold, English poet & critic.

London Photo 2016

A first-time encounter symbolizing 3 years of time-honored patience
and a slew of poems
and by the ritual of remembrance and I forget the words,
the stretched-out lines, there are so many.
So many times, a chance
would open up, a leeway in. And yet and yet
I sensed a closeness growing closer,
even a playfulness,
even *beyond beautiful,* I wanna say,
if such a realm exists.
Those meaningful coincidences unfolding surely.
Those sun-drenched afternoons,
those greyless graying skies & high contrasts, those puffy clouds,
a camera click.
A run for shelter from an April rain.
The laughter that ensues.
One take. It's in the script! It's in the telling.
A breezy holiday among the lonely plinths & swooping peregrines
and so much more that's merely guessing more redundancies.
Time is a risk.
The rest is scrambling to remember.
The rest is make-believe.
A laughter in the dark,
                         fading fading.

A photomatique strip more mellowed than yellowed.

      There's nothing of the legendary between us. No quick quip
in *Arts, Briefly* of the morning Times.
"Not a day hasn't gone by since..."
The phrase reminiscent of someone.
The movie evades me.
Where do all those cross-outs lead? The deletions.
The interruptions,
the gaps in time.
A gelatin print silvered
still holding secrets... or was it?
The innuendoes.
The gossips.
A name slips through the crevasse.
Whose emotions are recollected in tranquility?
Did Wordsworth's claim anticipate a future still unconscious?
Can words travel?
Today the Kaaterskills are silhouetted in a pale blue
with the golden hour soon descended,
filtered through a canopy of gossamers.
An archetypal Main Street frozen with its life in quietude.
There is no art that attests to this,
nor a color-tinted carte postale.
No revealing emails.
No working drafts.
No worlds adrift.
No one cares.
Sunlight flickered through the unfurled leaves.
It's winter now in Cornwall,
in St Ives,
on the northern coast
of the North Atlantic, and with a fog that lingers.
An array of sunsets.
A beauty to behold
bearing no resemblance to a lookalike
as testament to an emptiness.
A dream deferred,
imagining the absence of their sadnesses.

Gone

Did I ever tell you that moral codes are based on man-made *decisions...*
I guess not.
What would you do with an insight like this anyway?
How's that for a segue,
but in answering your last email
when you say, "I want to hear your voice,"
naturally I reply, 'I wanna see your face,'
the communiqués suddenly break off.
The ball's in your court, like they say,
but in all these summer months none appear
waiting when I open up the emails each morning.
Dead silence. A dead reckoning, like you don't exist
Niente! Niente!
like you're a make-believe beyond the predawn light
when dreams are still bewitched between 4 & 6.
Do you dream? Do you remember some of them?
Even your name begins to fade
& fade
& fade
        when the morning gets underway
and I feed the kitties with their hungry eyes
and the phone starts ringing and I don't pick up.
Chores done. I head out
for the morning *Times* and the morning poem
suddenly emerges across the obits page in my Mont Blanc script
of someone I once knew, also gone?
The morning's now at 102 degrees Fahrenheit
or when a coupla flashfloods
sweep down Union Street
like some "River of No Return"
once directed by Otto Preminger at his very best.

The New Mélancholia

      Someone, several maybe, will ask who's behind all this melancholy,
this insufferable state of mind affecting the heart also.
It's been years, I know.
Even I may have forgotten,
confused one name with another.
My Zazie, my principessa cat, might know.
She may've overheard a phone conversation with a friend.
But how do you talk through the language of a cat?
What to ask?
Otherwise, I'm at a loss.
And yet, and yet I can't seem to wanna let it go.
It's like some long lost thread unspooling and then it gets all tangled up.
It's like a dream that upon waking simply doesn't disappear,
but unable to reconnect where I left off,
and yet the dream continues, taking on its own *réalité*.
The missing link.
The missing name.
Or suddenly I'm on a no-name street.
Could it be Central London and not New York?
What's the city code,
the closest intersection,
the closest tube stop
that may provide a clue?
The only one at this point, I can imagine.
Cecil Beaton? Can't reach him. He's gone, or he would've told me.
This is getting me nowhere fast.
Even the poem is telling me, *I told you so.*

mélancholia 2

It's funny you'd given me the gift of mélancholia.
Had it not been for you,
I wouldn't have been able to ID the symptoms.
A slowness of breath, perhaps,
a flutter of a summer breeze passing through the open window.
A thought which is no thought but some sort of *ennui*.
A lingering, a malaise.
A forgetfulness, if even that.
Even a weekend in the countryside or along some long forgotten seashore
turns out not a remedy,
but more a longing or reminder of an emptiness I can't put my finger on.
Those puffy British clouds blanketed by sunlight
you'd see backdropped in some British flick.
The sky a rich, deep blue, though it's all in black & white.
The history knows not what the poems refer to.
The longing & the lingering.

The day after Friday, the 13th...

...but wch month? The further I get from you, the more poems get written.

That's the way it's gonna be.

That's the fait accompli.

The deep blue sky contrasting those puffy flying clouds past the rolling foothills.

A slight breeze wafting in. A slow hello but no-hello.

The more poems naming you & claiming you but not exactly naming you, my dear.

You're not *my dear.* Not yet the human heart.

What's the odds even passing you, a rainy striding street

in Mayfair London, the stopping & the stare

those shoppe windows taking in the gloom, the nonchalant *histoire,*
                                        those reflective glares

that go the way of endnotes unaccounted for. A Namib mirage?

How's that come to be an endnote or a clue?

Who's counting anymore? Who's fooling who?

Where's your crazy mind been all these dusty years? How many crazy years?

photomatiques

There are still some names barely visible in the active files
or how you used to look,
and yet the facts remain scrambled, unintentional.
So that what was known about you in my inner life
becomes obscured even further, darker,
like my Pentel suddenly runs outta ink.
                              Ack!
I reach into my pocket for a pencil stub, a No. 1 it turns out,
and suddenly my mindset shifts to a redeemable truth.
Photographs don't lie--that's the myth
purported, such as an innocent rendezvous
clowning 'round until all sense of time's lost in those strips of film--
a photomatique brought back to life, as fate would have it.
Those smiles of spring belie a certain mélancholia,
an affliction of the mind & heart
defining the malaise,
my own unexpected dilemma.
The unexpected parting of the ways
Where are those ways now undocumented?
Is there an ending that continues unrelenting with an "n.d." compressing time?
Is your name forever eradicable,
or simply make-believe the way life can be a make-believe also.
The histories made up.
The Cornwall hikes,
                    the sundown holidays, the birder interludes.

J'attendrais

       Why do I have to die in order to remember that I lived?
is a line that lingers
when I woke
and still holds no meaning.
Stillborn
in the very words, the syllables,
long passages, the mélancholia
waiting in the wings.
The many months of silences still to be explained, identified.
Better get a move on.
Cocteau's *Astonish me!*
My cats astonish me, all curled up
and sleeping deep beside me.
Dreaming also, I suppose. All those
little twitches.
This poem's getting off to a slow start. I can feel it.
Still sluggish from the long drive home from the city
whence I bought my *Schott.*
The same jacket Marlon Brando wore causing havoc in *The Wild One.*
Those darknesses at noon.
Those times I'd be drifting off
where a dream or two awaits me, or maybe none at all.
All those stock phrases one too many. What to do?
Not the havoc in my life that I recall.
The list long & long but not the havoc.
I follow my nature to be happy, more likely. You ask, "Can that be?"
Poems more likely. Lots & lots of poems.
Nothing's taken for granted,
filling in the gaps so memories are clueless, seamless.
                                     Nothing's unaccounted for.

The New Mélancholia 3

    The skylight was unlike any other.
A greyless grey. Had it been
a sun-filled day,
the setting would've been all wrong.
It wasn't up upon the moors.
A thatched cottage in the wilds of Dorset.
Stretches of empty beach for miles around
or the lei lines lost among the thickets
or somewhere in windy Cornwall with the winding bushy paths.
It was right here in New-York hyphenated
where I grew up.
The Bronx specifically.
I could hear the subway's roar beneath my feet
unlike the Tube, the Underground.
No bright lights there.
A dream slowly evaporating, so very far away,
like the slow fade of a forgotten movie still fading, fading...
and then all was gone.
                  I found myself alone suddenly
with this feeling I couldn't name.
Was it a faery tale, a pixie? The shadows deepening?
Not even poetry could name it.
Just the memory of emptiness like an Irish rain...
and then I woke... and what has ended?
There's no way to stop & start a sleeping dream.

The New Mélancholia 4

You've given mélancholia a bad name, but how could that be?
It's always had a bad name.
It's just that you appeared in the wrong century
when the moors had quieted down, the wolves asleep
and the howling winds lessened
and the window-frames stopped creaking rattling back & forth
in the middle of an autumn's chilly night,
or in those later afternoons even, a greyless grey
when an unexpected apparition would show up.
A stranger at the door.
Were you that unexpected visitor?
Were you in your own way totally unique for the part
with that flirtatious look,
the intelligence inventing beauty,
or was it the other way around?
It's all so unexpected, so confusing.
You've been part of this century
nearly 200 years now
from when the traditions got underway
and letters were written, hand-delivered, I would imagine.
Parfumed to the touch.
Cursives scrolled by quill of the rarest kind.
A poem here and there.
Have you been hanging out with the Lake Poets again,
with Coleridge & with Wordsworth?
What do you talk about to while the time away?
Or are you just part of the local gentry?
It had to be English. It couldn't have been French.
Their ennui was even more challenging to the psyche, more secluded.
You were too outgoing for the French.
You were a legend in your own time, but what is your time?
I've had my imaginings.
I've even had my childhood curiosities and astonishments. How's that?!
But I hadn't expected the likes of you!
I hadn't expected you in this day & age, that you
could behave in such & such a way becoming finally an anima!
Here one second, gone the next
and nothing that could prefigure the happenstance of who you were.
I've never known mélancholia or where it comes from,
what it does to the mind,
the heart also,
and all the rest a malaise of sorts.
My joints all achy.

Those dreams ahead become an avalanche.
The love & then some.
The heart suspended in its disbelief.
A casual description of this morning's weather.
                              The twilight's last gleaming.

Nicola darling,
              Is it memory loss to the first ever meeting back in 2016
and in the back-and-forth dailyness of what's remembered after all?
The yours & mine.
The years between & inbetween.
A wavelength of emotions,
your one sudden candid burst revealing much:
                              "Something blocks me...
perhaps, the instability of it all."
It's not hard contemplating those broad London
darkened streets you'd traversed in schooldays past,
now absent of your walking presence, your tinselled strides!
You took the other way round & missed the shot.
There's no such emotion as impatience without the hand-held camera
                                proving otherwise.
No instance of your childhood: where that would lead you
in these dreams darkened
by the rushing swirling Cornwall clouds.
You never ask & there's historically no answer.
No instance describing how a photograph can overwhelm you.
Where is the *outrenoir* in you like the texture in an uncut grass.
Tomorrow or today? There are no sequels.
                    What's left?

Approaching London on Virgin flight 010, 20:XI:19

When I experienced this sudden nothingness I had no name for,
except for your long afternoon farewell,
there's no way you could've known this,
seeing you skipping past the mallards on the Pond in Central Park.
Past the Tavern on the Green with its varied histories,
the gossips lingering,
the all-nite bashes.
But this was not what I'd been seeing in the trailing fading 60 seconds or so,
and then I turned away,
and where
you headed you didn't say,
and the rain hadn't kept its promise.
Instead a greyless gray blanketing the skies,
except for so much more I meant to say but hadn't.
Some other day not to be repeated,
but it's been a year if I'm not mistaken,
someday maybe more.
The afterglow of what it would've been.
Suddenly the overcast remained just so, closed in
because the gods had willed it thus.
Wch gods? Wch way is so confusing to the heart & mind?
But there it was.
                    And that's the gist of it.

après for Time

Even in dreams there's happiness. Even the undreamt.
The happenstance of winter.
Those Great Plains in a sheering snowstorm,
confined for weeks on end, even months.
Some cotton sheets fluttering in a noonday breeze,
imbued with scented sunlight.
Those far fields, the wintry skies abound, still lingering.
The stories that remain alleged, so what?
How to share them?
The nomenclature entwined, chronological.
The fotos say so.
Yet so few remain.
The dark & handsome happy smiles prove otherwise.
The goofy playfulness in a basement-buried photobooth.
Still, what happened? Who were they,
wrestling for each other's soul without seeming to?
Yet neither lived to see the day. The poems say so.

                              The poems could be wrong.

Skimpy remembrances

     The first time I spoke to you, in 2016, was at Somerset House during its annual Photo London
exhibits. Don't you recall?
The weather was balmy
as you leaped from one booth to another
with your Oxford entourage in tow.
In the need to know
would come a day later in fragments.
We introduced each other through our smiles, our eyes
and then through our hands
when you clasped mine in a clasping warmth not letting go.
It's as if you'd chosen me.
We didn't talk much.
When we did,
only brief exchanges, etc. of our past emerged
while "minding the gap"
to some tube stop. I'd forgotten the name if there was any.
The time-tables all lit-up LEDS & frozen.
And around us time was everywhere frozen,
and time was all I had left. I left first,
like the sifting of sands
through open hands
and three-thousand miles of insuperable ocean
trying not to look back as I passed through the doors.
And yet the poems continued unabated, like an unsettled storm
veiled with an absence
in place of your presence.
3 years later you're elsewhere. There's more.
The sun floated in the hazy lazy London skies,
half-tinted gray in its aspects. A dusk was descending.
The words also floating,
                      then no more.

Dream waking...

     In my sleep I'm rising into the late afternoon wintry light
forgetting nothing
of everything
I have forgotten.
The list is infinitesimal. Have I pronounced it right?
And there are names names I've forgotten.
Incidents that lead through one door to another.
What have I left behind?
Have I left my life behind? How far back
do I dare go?
Will I lose touch
with much?
Hello! Hello! Can you hear me?
No one answers.
No one answers back.
Where have everyone gone?
I am following a labyrinth
and there's this dead-end
and I've to start from scratch.
I need to give my legs a rest.
I need to sit down a while,
a bench, a slab of stone, a rock.
That's not too much to ask,
but no one's hearing me.
I'm nearing the one year stretch when I last saw Nicki in New York.
Has it been that long?!
She made a point of saying she'd be back
before the year is out.
Maybe even a few months shy of that.
And now she emails me to say she's stranded somewhere in Pennsylvania,
and now she doesn't say where with whom.
What am I to make of this?
Is this getting to be a maze of dreams?
I can't make head or tail what's going on here.
Why all this meshugass happening?
The wilds of Pennsylvania.
A family heirloom,
A painting by one Samuel John Peploe,
one of the Scottish Colorists.
I tell her to sell it! Unload!
I'm getting a bit winded here.
A lot of words can do it when they don't connect.
There's no way to sort this out.
I'm standing in the middle of nowhereland.

No. Wait. I'm lying up in bed with paper, pen
trying to balance all this out
and still I'm further from where all this began,
and now there's less time left,
and what's left is even more forgetful, frightful.
I'm back in my bedroom with my Duchamp cabinet
And the bedside clock lights up 4:22. How coincidental,
but it's not a.m., it's p.m.
This is the wrong time to be dreaming!
I should be asleep,
yet I can hear Sasha in the next room me-owing & me-owing
and now he's suddenly on my lap
providing comfort with his glowing Cheshire eyes.
My breathing seems easier now.
It gets dark earlier this time of year.
Soon my slumbering will reach me.
                    Soon I'll feel safe again in sleep.

Poems 2016-2019

They were written in Hudson from 2016 through the end of '19,
                                        and they depict
a longing & an unsung ensuing mélancholia.
A "mélancholia" shifting the parameters of any block of time
dating back to the early 19th century
when an everyday of contrasty clouds passed over tarns & crags & fells
where William Wordsworth & his nearest neighbour for a while
                                Coleridge once lived,
writing well into those dawning lights by candlelight.
This was not Paris in the 1920s, '30s, '40s.
The ambiance was somehow new & unexpected.
No Café Flore here.
No Saint-Germain-des-Près across the way.
These were overlapping images of cobblestones, wrought-iron lampposts,
canopies & awnings billowing along the Oxford Street.
A sole encounter, one of many, lost among the swirls
of intermittent rains.
The whir of cabs.
The open markets far & few between.
The shopping at Liberty's, had it happened.
Lunch & a pot of Earl Grey.
The poems cloudlike, steamy, in their rising ambiance,
their remaining drafts.
                        Why do these things happen?

Dear Nicola, Nicki for short

Dear Nicola,
    Clearing out the clutter from my office this lone wintry day,
I came upon a receipt, actually 2 receipts--we split the check--
for the one & only lunch
we ever had, The Smith
across from Lincoln Center.
You had the Avocado Toast, I had the Tagliatelle,
2 Cappuccinos each,
and where we discovered astonished
a photomatique in the basement--how fated is that?!--
where we lost all sense of time
like 2 kids in a candy store
for nearly an hour's worth of frolicking posing
all those crazy poses
that should last a hundred years or so,
and then you walked me over to the Park
the Tavern on the Green,
to catch my ride home to the Kaaterskills,
& I sensed we'd never see each other again wch turns out mostly true
& worth at least another hundred years of memory outliving us
& add to that another hundred worth of poésie.
It's like we never really met
and all this clearly now imagined.
Recollections of a future never happening.
A weeklong jaunt to Cornwall,
the ocean spray,
the white-capped sea. Land's End.
The walk along the shoreline by no one.
Hands held round a mug hot chocolate in St Ives.
The present with those futures past filled with ghosts.
        Those moments unimaginable...

That's life

Nicola sweetheart,
                    Is that what Marcel Duchamp meant when he said phonetically
C'est la vie?
The Lord giveth and the Lord taketh away. Fuck that shit!
Who was I talking to?
It was Demetrio Paparoni, "Dem" for short,
distinguished fine art scholar, living in Milan.
...that we must be more clever, more vigilant
while even wearing gloves when turning doorknobs,
getting in & out of cabs,
or washing hands for up to 30-seconds.
In fact, I like washing my hands
for 30-seconds,
but don't need to be reminded.
I do it of my own volition.
I do it to honor you Nicola, on my birthday, 1st day of spring,
one of the innocents. Allow me. Come.
I do what I have to do to encourage you
to lift yourself outta bed,
step over to the big bay window with your camera,
behold the desert blooms before you, the rainbow garden now before you,
as all the varied vistas come into focus for your eyes only.
Let me guess, you said you're left-handed.
I'm left-handed too.
You see, I don't forget.
But for some unknown reason I'm also left-eyed
when focusing through the camera
and I imagine you are, too.
It makes a whole lotta sense
the way life brought us together when it did,
and the way life will astonish us, even more. That's life
with its many surprises,
its many camera angles,
its mysterioso points of light, its many stars in the firmament,
its many snapshots, many many lines of poetry.
Its many walks by the cresting surging sea,
or walking in the woods
as hosts of birds sing down to us their song
of life to you & mine hurrying along.
Each tree is the tree of life, a talking tree, many talking trees.
Many many talking trees.
They understand deep in their roots.
They shade us with their bending boughs.

Unfurl their shade to give us shade.
They throw the light prismatically.
Can you hear them now?

What are they telling us...
                                    telling us?

Look Homeward Angel

Howzit Nicola,
            There's been some skepticism about who you are
in these so-called poems,
that in my mind may have escaped. Ha-ha. Not true.
The cries & whispers
as Charles Ives' 4th Symphony spins out its "last mouvement,"
the dénouement, those brief fading fading notes
like a walk in the park,
that fragile twilight remains as secretive a gift
coming from this little boy
with always one of God's creatures lovingly nearby.
The winter coat he's wearing stitched by his dad Jerry
he'd be sewing well into the nite.
The austerity & love that went into it, fits me snug...
and then the camera clicked.
Did we visit
the reptile house?
Did we feed the elephants?
My favorite time,
imagine petting tigers on their head.
Gerard, wake up! Wake up!
The après this,
the après that.
Everything was swiftly turning like on a multi-colored carousel.
There's no more the question of our lucky stars
as in a circle still unbroken
nearly 4 years past.
We ask anyway.
Do I get to hug you now, or can I wait for all eternity?
Where are the simpler times... or were they?
These imaginings turned real with the decades yet to follow.
The synchronicities prophesied.
Time postponed, suspended.
Those labyrinths of time still ticking,
            and where to find you in the wordless April London mist.

Film noir letter to Nicola

Dearest Nicola,
               I never thought it would come to be this way,
like a blind date in life,
like waking up in the middle of the nite,
realize
it's getting on to dawn
with its uncertainties,
scarcities,
the superstitions, the cobbled streets
ghostlier than at any other time, that I recall.
That's how bad my memory slips my mind.
There are no El trains. It's all subways now.
No tellin' time anymore.
Every day a new day with a mindful little twist.
The line of scrimmage moves ever so slightly.
So the slightest misstep is a step into the dark.
Suddenly its existentialism turned on its head. Suddenly!
a throw of the dice *never never* will abolish chance
against a rusticated wall,
an elusive sand dune,
a beach of rotting ships,
a food concession closed.
If this be *verboten,*
then everything is.
The world shrunk to the eye of a needle.
It's the darkness at noon that lingers & still lingers.
Rififi was a French movie, I believe, by Jules Dassin.
Now it's for real. Rain is predicted.
Perhaps one picture will change the course of history.
You once remarked to me, "black & white is timeless." So it is.
That unexpected sneeze. *Gesundheit.*
My memory where we were having lunch is now a hunch.
                              I'm only kidding.

Time is now mute.
I miss your mythology, my mythology. Ha-ha.
I look at Zazie as she quietly stares into her water bowl.
Does she sense something all amiss?
8:10. It's already dark outside.
You nearly 4000 miles away
as the crow flies, give or take a few.

Brief Encounter

Darling,
          There was a time when Time, I would imagine,
stood still for you, as you stood still also
for your dad's family camera.
The mid-80s, I would imagine... a holiday
about right.
Wide-eyed as was the child in you
framed by those straight drugstore edges, slightly cropped.
Color was the thing,
as I imagine you staring through the snapshot
when I caught your eye,
your innocent, infectious smile.
What did you say to me? Eternities
separated us,
but you nor I knew that.
The old world & the new. Was there a beach near you?
A children's zoo?
A coloring book filled with tygers & giraffes?
Have you forgotten these & them?
I could imagine, as I imagine
now: Does it ever cross your mind
to wanna turn back in Time
to wish upon a star, to dream a rainbow's end?
Recapture all those dreams, some half-forgotten. Wazit?
What was the first time you held a camera to your eye?
What did you see you might've missed
as days gone by?
A sand dune. A duststorm. A herd of desert elephants.
I may've said this all before some roundabout way or other.
That's what poetry is like.
Is *like what?*
It's like everything & nothing.
                              The curfews of a life.
Is like words & words & words, & sure enough
a poem gets in the way, stands up & walks.
I'm tip-toeing in the dark.
I await the dawning golden light.
There's an overcast. There's rain a comin'.
It's day for nite.
Curiosity is the borderline.
You say "I want to see your face."
'I wanna hear your voice,' near & far.
                              Wake up.
Can you hear me
now? Can you? Can you?

April 11th 2019

    April 11th would've been the 1st anniversary if there was one.
The words seem forever out of reach.
Like who cares?
Nothing happened.
The early afternoon was more illuminating.
The sky a bright greyless gray.
Once you cleared the hill in Central Park, all was gone.
Nothing to describe
or the absurdity of life
or NYC from an unexpected late snow that doesn't seem to wanna stick.
I had to look closer to remember.
The trees had not yet leafed,
but the curbs were swept.
At that moment, I awoke to a blinding sunlight
along a coast that stretched in both directions all at once
for hundreds, hundreds of miles of deserted, uncluttered beach.
And then off in the distance
I saw a silhouette of a figure moving slowly in my direction
and at first I couldn't make out who it was...
And then I saw...
I could not believe my eyes.
I cried out to you above the din.
                Howzit, howzit.
There was no response.
You kept on walking, almost struggling in the dune,
and then you finally came close enough & stopped.
                       Is that you?
I couldn't make out what you were saying.
The wind was deafening, stifling,
and yet everything around me felt comfortable, peaceful.
Even the waves had lost their sound.
You turned your face sideways to the backlit glare
falling on your face, the bridge of your nose.
You clenched your fist as if biting into it
and holding back the tears... It was an old photograph,
                       a snapshot really.
We stood quietly for a few moments,
as meaningless as a passing dream.
You took the pose & stepped into it.
I heard you stirring.
I heard the waves waking, in the distance. A lulling sound...
And then nothing, nothing.
               There was nothing.

NOTES

COVER: *Chiswick trees dedicated to Jean Wainwright, Sunday, November 24th 2019.*

It couldn't have been more fated than a late night's rainfall when for the morning after as I was on my way to the local café just down the road from Jean's house I stumbled upon this immense spread of standing water at the corner filled with upside-down trees that nearly caused a dizziness within my frame of vision. I knew then & there I must photograph this miracle of nature for the cover of my next book of poetry; and so ran back to the house to fetch my Nikon and capture it all in a matter of 5 minutes from every conceivable hypnotic angle until the film ran out. I owe this all to Jean's support & inspiration for the work I've done & the enthusiasms we've shared along the way during the many fun times she's hosted my presence in Chiswick & in London.

"The Lives They Lived" is the title of the year-end supplement for the Sunday *Times* and is cited here with the kind permission of *The New York Times.*

Even before I embarked on compiling nearly 4 years of work for this volume, I knew instinctively that every poem included here would have to be a hit out of the park, to steal a baseball term. In this instance, I single out only M. Marcel Proust as the central influence with how these poems came to be.

COLOPHON

The New Mélancolia & Other Poems was published by Bottle of Smoke Press in March 2021.

The text is set in Garamond Premier Pro Roman, Bold, & Italic. Garamond Roman and Bold was based on the design of Claude Garamont (c. 1495-1561) and the italics were based on the design of Robert Granjon (1530-c. 1590).

Published in an edition of 2000 copies bound in paper covers & 26 hardcover copies (A-Z), each signed by the author and containing a tipped-in, silver gelatin photograph of Gerard Malanga signed by the photographer.

Made in the USA
Middletown, DE
08 March 2021